A Masque of Poets

A Masque of Poets

of Poets

George Parsons
Lathrop

MINT EDITIONS

A Masque of Poets was first published in 1878.

This edition published by Mint Editions 2021.

ISBN 9781513212135 | E-ISBN 9781513212036

Published by Mint Editions®

 **MINT
EDITIONS**

minteditionbooks.com

Publishing Director: Jennifer Newens
Design & Production: Rachel Lopez Metzger
Project Manager: Micaela Clark
Typesetting: Westchester Publishing Services

Take this to heart, O Poets of Today,
And let it give you comfort on your way:
A single verse may live as long, God please,
As all of Shakespeare or Euripides.

Contents

A Song before Singing

Sing! sing of what? The world is full of song;
    And all the singing seems but echoed notes
Of the great masters who, when souls were strong,
    Rolled sturdy pæans from rejoicing throats.

Or worse than echoes, schemes of tinkling sound,
    The pilfered phrases of the melodist,
A bastard music, a tenth Muse discrowned,
    A light bewildered in a blinding mist.

I would not dabble on the brink of power,
    Shape airy nothings, dreaming of a dream,
Chime word with word, and pipe to catch the hour,
    But plunge, aim-certain, in the living stream.

Give me a theme to sing in man's behoof,
    As full of purpose as my faith, O God!—
Red with our life-blood, firm in warp and woof,
    A homely product of the common sod.

Or else, let silence and primeval night
    Reign, as God reigned within his holy dark,
Eons on eons, till he called the light,
    And the first poet wakened with the lark.

"If only we had Time to spare"

If only we had time to spare
    To taste the glories of the Spring,
How good to leave this noise and glare,
And breathe the blessèd country air,
    And hear the songs the wild birds sing,
If only we had time to spare!

Then you should stretch you at my feet
    And read aloud, and I should sew,
And now and then our eyes might meet,
And we might murmur phrases sweet
    And blissful hours would come and go
If only we had time to spare!

But as you toil, and as I pray
    For happier and idler hours,
Noon follows dawn, night follows day,
I look, and lo, your locks are gray
    And Winter withers up our flowers
Ere ever we have time to spare!

LALAGE

When I have kissed the Rose upon the path
    And loved her, touch to touch and eye to eye,
The joy I have of her I know she hath
        For every passer by—
        What right have I?

Wakes in my heart the morning of thy speech,
    Sings in my soul the music of thy smile,
And thou'rt as far as Roses out of reach—
        For in a little while
        Will they beguile

Hearts, not my own, of other sorrowing—
    Ah, and thy voice's music, sweet and low
And gentle with all magic of the spring
        Shall touch them even so—
        Do I not know?

I know it well, and yet in peace I part!
    I know God made the Rose, and gave to thee,
To help his whole wide world, the Rose's heart,
        Nor left thy bounty free
        To pluck by me.

Awakening

Well—I said, it is all too true
The story told to my childish ears,
That tears were many and joys were few,
And hopeless the weight of gathering years.
I never believed a word of the tale,
And turned to the sun and rejoiced in the day,
But a blow struck home and the light grew pale
Till bitter darkness beset the way.
Oh, what is it all? (I pondered),—what
This terrible life wherein we are set
Defenceless, whether we will or not;
Where the swift years weave us a golden net
Of joys so sweet and of hopes so bright,
Only to rob us day by day,
Slowly to take from the eyes their sight,
Steal all the body's senses away,
And deal to the soul such blows of loss
Through the hand of Death?—and there I ceased,
For a wave too bitter rolled across,
And a longing never to be appeased
Shook me with sorrow beyond all thought.
Outside I heard the spring wind sigh,
As if the pathos of life it caught,
And strove to utter it, wandering by.
When, in a moment, the door swung wide,
Sunshine and flowers and songs of birds
Swept in with you like a golden tide,
Sweetness and rapture too deep for words.
O Love, you brought to me youth and spring,
Took me by storm with a glad surprise;
And set my whole soul worshipping,
And saved my life with the look in your eyes!
And while you are left to me, no more
Can my heart be dull as a senseless clod,
While you hold me fast with those eyes so sure,
Humbly I reach for the hand of God.

Benedicam Domino

Thank God for Life. Life is not sweet always,
Hands may be heavy-laden, heart care-full,
Unwelcome nights follow unwelcome days;
And dreams divine end in awakenings dull,
Still it is life, and life is cause for praise.
This ache, this restlessness, this quickening sting,
Prove me no torpid and inanimate thing,
Prove me of Him who is of life the spring:
I am alive,—and that is beautiful.

Thank God for Love; though Love may hurt and wound,
Though set with sharpest thorns its rose may be;
Roses are not of winter, all attuned
Must be the earth, filled with soft stir, and free
And warm ere dawns the rose upon its tree.
Fresh currents through my frozen pulses run,
My heart has tasted summer, tasted sun;
And I can thank Thee, Lord, although not one
Of all the many roses blooms for me.
Thank God for Death. Bright thing with dreary name;
We wrong with mournful flowers her pure still brow;
We heap her with reproaches and with blame:
Her sweetness and her fitness disallow
Questioning bitterly the why and how.
But calmly 'mid our clamor and surmise
She touches each in turn, and each grows wise,
Taught by the light in her mysterious eyes,—
I *shall* be glad, and I am thankful now.

Provençal Lovers

Aucassin and Nicolette

Within the garden of Beaucaire
He met her by a secret stair;—
The night was centuries ago.
Said Aucassin, "My love, my pet,
These old confessors vex me so!
They threaten all the pains of hell
Unless I give you up, ma belle";—
Said Aucassin to Nicolette.

"Now, who should there in Heaven be
To fill your place, ma très-douce mie?
To reach that spot I little care!
There all the droning priests are met;—
All the old cripples, too, are there
That unto shrines and altars cling
To filch the Peter-pence we bring";—
Said Aucassin to Nicolette.

"There are the barefoot monks and friars
With gowns well-tattered by the briers,
The saints who lift their eyes and whine:
I like them not,—a starveling set!
Who'd care with folk like these to dine?
The other road 'twere just as well
That you and I should take, ma belle!"
Said Aucassin to Nicolette.

"To Purgatory I would go
With pleasant comrades whom we know,
Fair scholars, minstrels, lusty knights
Whose deeds the land will not forget,
The captains of a hundred fights,
True men of valor and degree:

GEORGE PARSONS LATHROP

We'll join that gallant company,"—
Said Aucassin to Nicolette.

"There, too, are jousts and joyance rare,
And beauteous ladies debonair,
The pretty dames, the merry brides
Who with their wedded lords coquette
And have a friend or two besides,—
And all in gold and trappings gay,
With furs, and crests in vair and gray";—
Said Aucassin to Nicolette.

"Sweet players on the cithern strings
And they who roam the world like kings
Are gathered there, so blithe and free!
Pardie! I'd join them now, my pet,
If you went also, ma douce mie!
The joys of Heaven I'd forego
To have you with me there below,"—
Said Aucassin to Nicolette.

MY LADY'S VOICE

My lady dear hath so divine a voice
    That, when she speaks, all Nature must be mute,
    For in this low, soul-thrilling, delicate lute,
Nature's most sweetest harmonies rejoice,—
The very birds are hushed, in happy choice.
    And when she sings, the glorious Cherubim,
    And all the host of white-robed Seraphim,
And all the holy Elders, midst Heaven's joys
Rapt with an unknown peace, to list the strain
Do cease their silvery harps, and kneel attent,
Wondering now first to know God's smile in sound.
E'en the sad doomed forget th' eternal pain,
While, thro' the gates of Paradise, out-bent,
Heaven throngs to Earth, where bliss doth so abound.

Through a Window Pane

A Winter Memory

That bright December morning,
    Playfully, by the pane
She lingered;—for ever blossom,
    Sweet morning, in heart and brain!

With arch farewell she lingered,
    Her face through the frost-bloom bright,
Smiling;—like frost-bloom vanished
    That vision into the light!

For ever and ever, smiling,
    Through me it steals again:
Within my soul the picture
    Looks through my heart, the pane!

A Mood of Cleopatra

Cleopatra, when the chilling fear
Of ruin touched her soul at ease,
When turbid sounds, blown overseas,
Would speed on rumor's rapid path
From the hot lips of Roman wrath
Straight to her own Egyptian ear,—
Then, even at some grand feast of hers,
Would seem to feel the joy struck dumb
Of citherns, harps, and dulcimers,
With rumbling prelude, harsh to hear,
Of that which must in time become
Disaster, slavery, Actium!
Then she, that mighty and mystic queen,
Round whom her vassals crawled in awe,
Whose lifted finger was a law,
Whose smile an edict, and whose frown
A darkness on the lands between
Arabian wave and Libyan dust,
Whose name, tyrannic and august,
From marble-famed Syene's town
On wings of wonderment flew down
The old sacred Nile and serpentine,
North to Canopus and the sea;—
Cleopatra, couched at feast, even she,
Would quiver with a sudden sigh,
And one imperious hand would raise,

That bade the exultant music die,
And made, along its mighty maze
Of columned galleries, grandly high,
A silence as of death to come
On all the vast triclinium.

"If I must die," her thought would say,
"What way shall be the swiftest way?
What subtle drug shall give release
With slightest pain before it slay,
And make my conqueror find me here
As one who thrids, in cavernous night,
Some hypogëum's halls austere,
Expecting when his steps shall cease
Beside the uncrumbled cryptic peace
Of still sarcophagi, and when
He shall behold, with sharp delight,
With thrills of greed he shall behold,
The royal mummies lying rolled
In lordliest wealth against his sight,
Richly embalmed, these kings renowned,
In naphtha and bitumen bound:
But now he gains their bourne of sleep,
And sees their gilded coffers rise,
Stript of all wealth to clutch and keep,—
Plundered and spoiled ere this by those
Who have dared, in violative wise,
To assault with strong and impious blows
The awful, slumbering Pharaohs:—
Thus even shall he that finds me here
Find ruin of what I was alone,
The dumb bulk left, the life outflown
Beyond all shadow of shame and fear,
Since death can do whatso he please
With whoso he shall choose to strive,
But Roman hands, though quick to seize,
Can never manacle alive,
With wrist-gyve or with ankle-gyve,
The daughter of the Ptolemies!

"Wherefore, if I must die one day,
 How fleetest shall this flesh get peace?
What way shall be the swiftest way?
What subtle drug shall give release
With slightest pain before it slay?"

Then would she clap her small swart hands,
And soon the obeisant slaves would bring
Rare cups and goblets oddly wrought
With sculptured shapes in circling bands,
Or many a strange hieratic thing
Whereof these latter times and lands
Know either vaguely or know naught,—
With Athor, Isis, one-armed Khem,
Snake, scarab, ibis, wingèd ball,
Quaint Coptic anaglyph; and all
These vessels, to the brims of them,
With deadliest poisons had been fraught.

Then slowly through the hall's great space,
Where, statued in weird hybrid gloom,
The mighty basalt sphinxes loom,
With black claws crossed in cold repose;
Between the pillars huge of base—
That might bear heaven, if so they chose,
On bulging chapiters that enthrone
Colossal lotus-leaves of stone,—
Before the Queen, with timorous pace,
With groundward brow and quivering limb,
With horror on each haggard face,
They come, the slaves that are to die
Beneath Cleopatra's critic eye,
And pleasure thus her sovereign whim.

They dare not make one lightest moan
While ranging in a dreadful file
Before their slayer's icy smile.
They dare alone to cower and shrink;
Alone they dare to obey; alone

To grasp their goblets and be dumb;
For tortures worse than death might come,
Did they rebel in prayer and groan.
Some sweat with anguish as they drink;
Some totter, and have bristling hair;
Some choke their bitter sobs, and some
Roll eyeballs awful with despair!

Poisons are here of taste and hue
Most differing, yet all strong and fleet;
For here is Hellebore, Aconite,
Henbane, and Hemlock; Nightshade, too,
Opium, Euphorbia; these, and more
Known only in the years of yore.

And all are drunken to the lees
By those poor minion lips accurst.
A fearful quiet falls at first
Over the doomed ones where they stand,
Till now they sink, by sure degrees,
Form after stricken form, beneath
The smile so fathomlessly bland
Of the calm Queen who hears and sees
Their anguish of the stiff crooked hand,
The writhen body and gnashing teeth,
The blackening tongues, the crimsoned eyes,
The foamy and bloated lips, the cries
That up those monstrous galleries ring,
In mad debauch of suffering!

Superb doth Cleopatra sit,
The fragrant feast-flowers on her hair,
And o'er the shadowy waves of it
Her crown, imperially fair
For spikes of gold about the brows.
The delicate schenti that allows
Glimpses of her voluptuous shape,
Doth her firm bend of bosom drape,
And lightlier lies on her brown limbs

Than on some moonlit mountain's base
The gauziest vapor-wreath that swims.
From either side her languorous face
The fringy calisiris flows.
A gorget girds her olive throat,
Fantastic, beautiful to note,
Where clear-green chrysoberyl glows
Beside azedarac, in rows.

One marvellous arm supports her head,
With dull gold six times braceleted,
As backward on the empurpled ease
Of her Greek couch she leans at rest.
Her deepening smile hath half confest
That one thing yet holds power to please
Her tired soul, pleasure-surfeited;
One thing: this riot of death she sees,
This pomp of human pangs unblest,
This revel of ghastly agonies!

And so while at her feet they writhe,
While, levelled of their torture sore,
They grovel on the porphyry floor,
These slaves whose life is almost less
In Egypt than to crush a gnat,
Then (merciless change to wonder at!)
Cleopatra's smile turns bright and blithe,
Her eyelids lose their heaviness,
Her long deep eyes begin to shine,
And reaching one dark faultless hand
Where the gold festal goblets stand,
Carved by Lysippus' rare finesse
In sculptures worthy hands divine,
For veriest joy her red mouth laughs
As now, with back-flung head, she quaffs
The odorous white Mareotic wine!

GEORGE PARSONS LATHROP

LOVE AND FATE

I

Wry Fate denies me joy,
    But Venus' boy
Still strings my heart-strings to his bow:
They thrill whene'er his arrows go.
    O Fate, how can I view thee?
    O Love, how still pursue thee?

II

Though Love, indeed, be master,
    Fate follows faster
And snares us slyly from behind
Ere yet Love's distant goal we find.
    O Fate, how can I view thee?
    O Love, how still pursue thee?

Carpe Diem

Oh! today is too delicious,
Fill'd with little winds and birds
And the far-off hum of herds,—
Come, let's put off cruel words
This one time that Time's propitious.

Oh! today is too delicious.
Just this one most perfect day,
Let's forget while yet we may,
Let's love sorrow quite away,
Let tomorrow be malicious.

YOUTHFUL LOVE

I

Being absent, yet thou art not wholly gone,
For thou hast stamped thine image on the world;
It shines before me in the blushing dawn,
And sunset clouds around its grace are furled.
Hast thou not burdened every summer breeze
With the remembered music of thy voice?
Sweeter than linnet's song in garden trees,
And making wearisome all other joys.
Sleep vainly strives to bar thee from his hall,—
Thou winn'st light entrance in a dream's disguise,
And there, with gentlest sway thou rulest all
His gliding visions and quick phantasies.
The busy day is thine; the quiet night
Sleeps in thy radiance, as these skies in light.

II

Or stooping toward me from the stainless sphere,
And reaching dearest hands of comfort down,
Thou guidest steps that falter on alone,
Through darkened ways. Do I not feel thee near,
And lightest whispers of thy spirit hear,
Clearer than yonder sea's eternal moan?
And ah! no breath of any mournful tone,
But lessons of high courage, holy cheer,
And such sweet notes as charm the snake Despair.
Shall it not be so? Doth poor Fancy err
To hear thee speaking through the rosy air
Of morn and eve, and when no cloud may stir
In the calm noon; or solemn Night and fair,
Plies her grave task, and the stars wait on her?

Sunset—song

I

See the sun's departing smile,
Sweetest maid!
Let us sit and rest a while
In the shade.
None can hear us, none can see,
But the birdling in the tree,
Sweetest maid!

II

Lay your soft white hand in mine,
Lillie dear!
Let my arm your waist entwine,
Do not fear;
For the birdling in the tree
Would not tell of you and me,
Lillie dear.

III

While the sun hangs dim and red
In the west,
Come and lean your wondrous head
On my breast.
It is sweet, my Lillie dear,
By your side while night draws near
Thus to rest.

IV

Hide, oh, hide those lips so fair
From my view!
Oh, the madness but to dare
If you knew!

But to see and not to dare,
Sweet my love, that surely were
Madness too.

V

Lo, the weary day has fled,
Dearest heart!
Through the dark crowns overhead
Night-birds dart.
Sleep the birdlings in their nest,—
Those who love each other best,
Yet, Love, must part.

To Alma

I

An anxious whisper steals unto my ear,
That thy young soul, so fresh and pure it be,
Is alien unto mine; that I in thee
No resonance shall find for thoughts austere;
No glorious kinship in that loftier sphere
Where spirits meet and recognize their own.
And yet, belovëd, from those depths unknown—
Those slumbering depths of silence which I fear
With my rude touch to stir—some shy sweet thought
Comes upward trembling, like a coral bright,
Which no bold eye its loveliness has taught,
Through pale green waters flashing its warm light!
Yet, wert thou shallow, love, the heaven's wide sweep
The shallow stream reflects, e'en as the deep.

II

Thy gracious face I greet with glad surprise
With each new day; and yet thou saidst a fear
Oft nestled at thy heart when I was near,
Because I loved thee only with mine eyes.
Thou wert not skilled in lore, nor deep, nor wise,
But thou wert strong to love and warm and true.
What could I answer, love? Alas, I knew
I love too well, perhaps, the radiant guise
Through which thy spirit breathes its loveliness.
Yes, darling, yes, I love thee as thou art,—
Thy coy surrender to my bold caress;
When folded in my arms, I feel thy heart
Beat 'gainst my breast; and when my lips meet thine
Thy very soul is wedded unto mine.

III

Yes, my old self is dead; and it is well;—
I knew, as thou, he had no right to be;
And light his death was, for he knew not thee,
And thrilling into life by some strange spell
I stood new-born and wondering; nor could tell
Aught of what had been. Through a mist outspread
I saw the by-gone years lie cold and dead,
And the bright future where with thee I dwell,
A happy Delos rising from the sea.
Dim seems my past and strange, and all the earth
A pale and melancholy pageantry,
Until the shining moment of thy birth.
Thy life from out this age of toil and gloom
Sprang, like a flower that blossoms on a tomb.

The Pine-tree

The Tree

Upward and ever upward,
    While the storms pass me by,—
Up through the lightning flashes
    Longingly look I.

The Flower

Yet when the storm-wind bloweth,
    Gentle pine-tree!
Downward thine arms in protection
    Stretchest thou o'er me.

The Tree

Upward and ever upward,
    While the sun rideth high,
Fearing not his bold glances
    Longingly look I.

The Flower

Yet when the sun's glance is hottest,
    Gentle pine-tree!
Downward thy poor child to shelter
    Leanest thou to me.

Husband and Wife

"Oh kiss me once before I go,
  "To make amends for sorrow;
"Oh kiss me once before we part
  "Who shall not meet tomorrow.

"And I was wrong to urge your will,
  "And wrong to mar your life;
"But kiss me once before we part,
  "Because you are my wife."

She turned her head and tossed her head
  And puckered up her brow:
"I never kissed you yet," said she,
  "And I'll not kiss you now.

"Tho' I'm your wife by might and right
  "And forsworn marriage vow,
"I never loved you yet," said she,
  "And I don't love you now."

So he went sailing on the sea,
  And she sat crossed and dumb
While he went sailing on the sea
  Where the storm winds come.

He'd been away a month and day
  Counting from morn to morn;
And many buds had turned to leaves,
  And many lambs were born,

And many buds had turned to flowers,
  For Spring was in a glow,
When she was laid upon her bed
  As white and cold as snow.

"Oh let me kiss my baby once,
 "Once before I die;
"And bring it sometimes to my grave
 "To teach it where I lie.

"And tell my husband when he comes
 "Safe home from sea,
"To love the baby that I leave
 "If ever he loved me:

"And tell him, not for might or right
 "Or forsworn marriage vow,
"But for the helpless baby's sake,
 "I would have kissed him now."

This Life of Ours

(A Song by the Way)

O Life of ours, when from thy grape
A poisoned vintage flows,
And to the whitened, cheated lips,
The wine a sinking comrade sips
A deadly gift bestows;—
O he will raise the murderous cup
With trembling hand that's loyal yet:
"Drink to this glorious life of ours,
Drink the dark wine fate grimly pours;
There is no terror but regret."

Regret and blame, they'll turn you tame!
O when a friend proves not a friend,
"Farewell" shall be the only word
By the sly listening demons heard;
And love's beginning soothe its end.
If eyes are harsh that once were kind,
And lips are proud that lately kissed,
O, let no faltering utterance show
The bitter inner overflow:—
We are not mourned unless we're missed.

Then life of ours, this life of ours!
Breathe her no coward sigh.
Is she a niggard of her hoard?—
She gives a title to a lord,
And to a knave, the lie.
But when along the misty hills
You see Grief coming, gray and cold
(Spear-armed like Pallas stern of old),
And when your heart with horror fills,
All-silent step before the breach,
Nor raise the brittle shield of speech
In parley; for thy doom is told.

Question and No Answer

Is it Ethics or Physics? Ah, that is the question:
Is it trouble of Conscience or morbid digestion?
Is the temper that makes all my family quiver
Ill-disciplined mind or disorder of Liver?
Does the Passion, that makes even wise men eccentrical
Proceed from the Heart? and if so from which ventricle?
Are duty and courage fine functions of Nerves—
Just as one horse goes steady, and another horse swerves?
Is the Genius that nature can hardly contain,
A film of gray marrow effused on the brain?
. . . Don't believe it, dear lady, or better, don't know it
But contentedly stick to your Parson and Poet.

Quatrains

The Money-Seeker

What has he in this glorious world's domain?
Unreckoned loss, which he counts up as gain;
Unreckoned shame, of which he feels no stain;
Unreckoned dead he does not know were slain;

What things does he take with him when he dies?
Nothing of all that he on earth did prize:
Unto his grovelling feet and sordid eyes
How difficult and empty seem the skies!

The Lover

He knows the utmost secret of the earth:
The golden sunrise's and sunset's worth;
The pregnancy of every blossom's birth;
The hidden name of every creature's mirth.

He knows all measures of the pulse's beat;
He knows all pathless paths of human feet;
He knows what angels know not of the sweet
Fulfilments when love's being is complete.

He knows all deadly soils where poisons bloom;
He knows the fated road where joy makes room
For nameless terrors and eternal gloom:
God help him in his sad omniscient doom!

On Appledore

Come thou with me, dear love, and see the day
Die on the sea, and o'er the distant land
This last faint glow of twilight fade away,
The while I hold in mine thy gentle hand.

The lessening light gleams on yon leaning sail;
Slowly the sun has sunk beyond the hill,
And sombre night in silence draws her veil
Over us two, and everything grows still.

Save when the tide, with constant ebb and flow
Of wandering waves that greet the steadfast shore,
Flashes fair forms of foam that falling throw
Their ardent arms round rocky Appledore.

Faint comes the cry of wild fowl in their flight
And chirp of crickets in the clover by,—
A meteor falls across the face of night
Sweeping its silver shower through the sky!

Or like the thread of a delicious dream
Some far-off sand-bird pipes its evening song,
While overhead the stars of Heaven beam
And bright Arcturus leads the sparkling throng.

Low whispering by us with a silent kiss
Comes the sweet south wind o'er the slumbering sea:
Thou dearest! can such a perfect joy as this
Be always mine, to drift through life with thee?

Jasper Oakes

The captain follows the sea no more,
But spends the eve of his days on shore;
And when about him an eager band
Beg for a tale of the sea or land,
The gentlest among them plead and coax
For the sad, strange story of Jasper Oakes.

———————

The ship was ready, the cargo stored,
The wind was willing, the crew on board,
And we sailed away from the English shore
For fair Manhattan, our home, once more;
But half way over, there came a blow
That threatened to sink us fathoms low.

The mate I shipped on the trip before
Was the bravest fellow on wave or shore,—
A thorough seaman, alert and wise,
And wondrous handsome, with fearless eyes,
A swift, sure foot and a steady hand,
A right good comrade on sea or land.

The jib swung loose in the sudden gale;
"Up," I shouted, "and furl the sail."
Before another could make reply,
The mate sprung forward and cried, "Aye, aye!
I am the oldest sailor here"—
"Stay!" I screamed in his heedless ear,

"Fasten a rope's end round you, then,
Even sailors are only men:
A dip of the boom will break your hold"—
"No!" he shouted, unwisely bold,
"Never a cowardly rope for me.
Tether a squirrel to climb a tree!"

The laboring vessel, with creak and strain,
Struggled and groaned like a thing in pain,
But Oakes, the bravest of all my men,
Never stood on the deck again:
Torn from his hold by the mad waves' might,
The wild sea swallowed him out of sight.

My gallant shipmate! I missed him sore,
And grieved as I seldom grieved before;
Yet, in my brooding, was glad to know
What he had told me a time ago,—
"I've not a tie in the world," said he,
"A ship is my sweetheart, my home the sea;

"And if I choke in the bitter brine,
Nobody's venture goes down but mine!"
So I rejoiced that no hearth was dim,
No fond heart broken, because of him,
That no sad woman would pine and wait
Or come and ask for the missing mate.

Past the Narrows and up the bay,
Home we came on a bright March day,
Glad of our harbor;—and, almost ere
The vessel touched at the well-known pier,
Lightly over the side there came
A slip of a girl, who called my name.

She had a face like an early rose,
And the smile of a child, who hardly knows
What the burden of living means—
Scarcely out of her happy teens—
"And who," I asked, "do you chance to be,
And what, my girl, do you want with me?"

"Only your mate"—with a smile more sweet,
"Your mate, my husband, I came to meet.
I could not wait, sir, a moment more;

I could not stay till he came on shore;
I hope"—she paused, and her face grew dim—
"I hope no evil has chanced to him?"

Stunned for a moment, I hardly knew
Whether my eyes and ears were true,
Yet there she stood, in her hopeful youth,
Her whole face earnest with love and truth,
Eager and anxious, with lips apart,
Waiting for news that would break her heart.

"Out on the jib-boom in a gale
He went in the darkness to furl a sail,
The vessel struggled and plunged and tossed—
The ropes were icy—and he was lost."
Bitter and cruel words, I knew,
But what could a clumsy sailor do?

Out of her face, in an instant white,
Vanished the glow, like a blown-out light,
The smile of joy and the beaming hope—
And down she dropped on a coil of rope,
Wringing her hands with moans of woe,
Like one struck down by a sudden blow.

The pitying sailors kindly bore
The poor girl-widow back on shore,
And the mate's sea-chest, and the little hoard
Of foreign trinkets he had on board;
But her poor pale face, with its grief and fright
Haunted my dreams for many a night.

With April's sunshine and breezes cool
We bowled back blithely to Liverpool,
And when at the close of a cloudy day
In front of its dingy wharves we lay,
Crossing the deck I chanced to see
A fair-faced woman, who asked for me.

No fresh young girl with a rosy face,
But a woman, wearing a matron's grace,
In whose soft eyes, as they questioned mine,
I saw the look of a mother shine;
And closely grasping her garment's fold,
Was a three-years' baby, with hair like gold.

With a chill that smote like a sudden blast
I thought of the woman who stood there last,
Sinking under her great despair;
And my glance grew into a startled stare,
As the boy came forward, and gazed at me
With the eyes of the man I had lost at sea.

"Where is Oakes?" asked a voice of doubt,
"Who sailed with you on the voyage out?
I am his wife—have I come too late?
Has he gone on shore? do you hesitate?
Speak to me, tell me! Ah, I see
You are keeping some terrible truth from me!"

Staggered, breathless—in dazed surprise
Under the spell of those well-known eyes,
Eyes which silenced my struggling doubt—
"Lost"—I gasped—"on the passage out—
Lost from the jib-boom—furling sail—
Overboard—in a heavy gale."

———————

Thus, as the captain quaffs and smokes,
He tells the story of Jasper Oakes.

Starlight

While the broad night above me broods,
In all her shadowy plenitudes,

I let my roaming vision fare
Through many an aisle of starry air.

"Bright throngs," I muse, "that o'er us bend,
How vague the messages you send!

"That fiery star, within whose rays
A wicked blood-red ardor plays,

"May be some world where dwell serene
A race with souls divinely clean!

"And that large tear of saintly light,
O'er the dead sunset throbbing white,

"Its snowy splendors looking, now,
Fit for some aureoled spirit's brow,—

"That star through ages may have been
Some great wild world that teems with sin!"

The Bunch of Wild Flowers

O Take this perfumed dewy offering,
    Not fairer than thyself, though wondrous bright,
Fanned by the woodland zephyr's balmy wing,
    At nature's kindly call, in sweet delight
Of their own beauty, these fresh wild flowers spring!—
    On what brown breezy moorland or green height,
In what cool sylvan glen or bosky dell,
Thou askest have I plucked them. I will tell!

Thou knowest the stream that through the meadows sweet
    And groves and gardens leaves the sunny plain
In a great silver coil, then hastes to meet
    Its high-born sister that speeds down amain
From the far summits to the mountain feet,
    And where they bounding join with murmuring strain
Of watery music, opes from plain and river
A gorge whose sides with leafy wildwoods quiver.

Into that gorge, like children to their home,
    At Maytide glad returning, down the hills
Clothed in light wreaths of pearl and silver foam
    And glittering in the sunlight, leap the rills;
Through its aerial depths the breezes roam
    Whispering mysterious language, and the bills
Of many birds make music in its woods
Answering the voices of the falling floods.

Of all these little crystal watery threads
    One most I love that, ere it tumbles down
Into the gorge, through a flat moorland sheds
    A linkèd light. There th' Iris lifts its crown
Of feathery gold and blue, and silver beds
    Of daisies gleam, and heather purple brown
And green fern deck its brink, and pearly floss
Of shining moor-flax and bright golden moss.

This morn at rise of sun, upon the bank
 Of that sweet brook, thinking of days gone by,
I slowly strayed, for there the heather drank
 Longsyne the blood of battle, there the eye
Of valor blazed, and there the conquered sank
 With no small meed of glory, for the sky
Ne'er looked on starker field as night came on
And the white moon on equal carnage shone!

There oft the shepherd's lonely footsteps pass
 By ancient graves forgotten, there his look
Not seldom met the cloven helm of brass
 And shivered sword-blade by the tumbling brook:
There riven corselets once gleamed 'mid the grass,
 And whitened skulls o'er which the red plume shook
In warlike pride upon that hapless day,
But all with time and rust have passed away.

And as I wandered on, anigh I drew
 Unto a spot where stood a fair Ash tree
Alone, new garmented in leaves wherethrough
 The morning zephyrs whispered blithefully
As if from some far heavenly place they blew;
 Around it spread a flower-enamelled lea,
And 'neath its shadow rose a small green mound
That heard alway the streamlet's lulling sound.

Upon that little height I sat me down
 And paused a while, and thought of those who slept
Beneath me, for I knew from old renown
 The story of their fate. Wellnigh I wept
To think of them. Thou knowest the ancient town,
 Upon the bending lowland stream, that kept
Watch on the passes, when of old the hand
Of baleful war uprose with reeking brand.

Beside the town there dwelt a lordly man
 Of lineage old, who had one daughter fair;—

Over her golden head twelve summers' span
    Had scarcely sped when on the meadows bare
Beside the stream, as civil strife began
    Her father met his foe, and blindly there
They fought and slew each other, and their gore,
Mingled together, stained the river shore!

And the foe had one son, a gallant boy,
    Born with high heart and hand, and friends would tell
The tale, well mixed with subtle hate's alloy,
    How on the fatal sward his father fell
And by whose hand, urging him to destroy
    The rival house, till one day in a dell
Beside her home they met, this youthful twain,
And 'stead of hate, love bound them in his chain!

And spite of warring friends on either side,
    Of death and ancient bickerings, year by year
Their love grew stronger, till in hope and pride
    Of youthful manhood he, without a peer
In all the land, besought her for his bride,
    And on light wings the bridal day drew near,
And women blessed them whose young hearts did prove
That feudal hate could never vanquish love!

But ere it came, the joyous bridal day,
    War's cloud had burst in wrath, the eager fife,
The rattling drum, the brazen clarion's bray,
    Were heard on all sides mustering for the strife;
And 'stead of marriage robe, the iron gray
    Gleamed o'er his breast, and filled with martial life
The long plume danced above his helmèd head
As from his loved one to the fray he sped.

Upon that moorland of the Stream and Tree
    The hostile ranks were marshalled face to face,
And each one darkly eyed his enemy
    And grasped his sword-hilt firmer, as the space
Grew narrower 'twixt the advancing lines, and he,

That soldier brave and young, in foremost place
Of the long ridge of battle, through the smoke
Upon the opposing ranks in thunder broke.

And as his fierce-eyed charger clove the press
    Of the thick spears in front, and he drew nigh
The foeman's standard, with quick watchfulness
    Mid the loud roar he marked a kindly eye
Bent on him with a look of sore distress,
    And a light nervous hand and sword raised high
To ward him 'gainst the frequent blows that came
On his proud head amid the dust and flame!

He knew that anxious eye, that lovely form
    Now armed and clad in warlike guise,—'twas she!
For to all daring deeds will true love warm
    Brave woman's heart! In dire extremity
She could not stay behind, and sought the storm
    Of battle by his side, and on that lea,
Alas! both fell together, as the day
Beyond the mountain summits died away!

Next morn the victors found them; on his breast
    Her young head lay in all its wealth and pride
Of golden locks, and peaceful was their rest,
    And painless seemed the breath wherewith they died.
Well the rough soldiers their sad story guessed,
    And buried them with reverence side by side,
On the flat moorland's fairest spot of ground,
And raised above their clay that little mound.

These flowers were culled around that hallowed spot:—
    Here are bright Violets wet with morning's tears,
And here cerulean blue Forget-me-not,
    And Hyacinth, for Constancy, that rears
Its head with Harebell by cool ferny grot,
    And Pimpernel that wakes the shepherd's fears
Of wind and rain, and Heartsease:—ah! they grew
Perchance above where closed her eyes of blue!

Here's Marygold for grief, and Celandine
    For bliss to come, and Primrose golden pale,
Emblem of youth, and Buttercups that shine
    For childhood's joy, and Cowslips of the vale,
Symbol of maiden grace, and dewy wine
    Of Johnswort that of old days tells the tale,
And Daffodils, the fairest of the fair,
Sprung from the spot touched by her yellow hair!

Here's delicate Anemone, that vain
    Stern Boreas wooed to his wide wastes of snow,
Here Daisies are for Innocence, for pain
    And pleasure mixed these sweet Wild roses blow,
With Moorpink washed by diamond summer rain,
    All sprung from where her beauteous cheeks lay low,
And this great blood-red flower that nature's art
Formed from the clay where mouldered his true heart!

With Ivy I have bound them fresh and green,
    Eternal symbol of Fidelity,
And Hawthorn blooms that tell of Hope serene,
    And with some leaves of that lone ashen tree
That whispers o'er their graves old songs which mean
    I know not what! Then take these flowers from me,
Born of the fruitful sun and mountain airs,
And think a while on love and what it dares!

Yachting

How the breezes bend and bow her,—
This frail yacht, that like a flower
    Overfloats the rolling foam!
Swift her sides the waters hiss on,
While yon calmer spaces glisten
    With the sunset's monochrome.

'Twixt the deeps of sky and ocean
Holdeth she her eager motion:
    So, between thy spirit's height
And my answering depth of passion,
My frail being seems to dash on,
    Buoyant, through the sunset-light!

A Quandary

Tell my lady she is fair?
    That no news is, truly.
Tell her she is sweet and rare,
    Pure and lovely past compare?
Will it strike her newly?

No, some other way to woo
    Must be found to win her.
What if I be fond and true?
    All the world adores her, too,
Such a spell is in her.

Ah, I have't! I'll stay away,
    Though I wander sadly;
Then, to say her gentle nay
    She must send for me someday,
And I'll go right gladly!

Don't Overdo it

I wonder whether
April-weather
Has taught you, lady, how to rule
My eager heart
With frolic art,
And keep it playing still Love's fool.

Your sunny breeze is
False, and freezes;
And when I think a freshening rain
Has come, the gust
Brings only dust,
And leaves me parched with barren pain.

A woman's favor
Loses savor
If it be yielded all too soon;—
'Tis very true.
But were I you
I'd heed the changes of the moon.

Your game is losing,
Though amusing.
Pray, have you seen an early bud
In spring unfold,
Then shrink with cold
And hide its blushing flower-blood?

In such a season
There's small reason;
And, though we sport with laughing May,
'Tis constant June
So fair and boon
That wins the flower and makes it stay.

Once overdo it,
And you'll rue it:
Too sharp a frost will kill, I fear.
The bloom you waste
Can't be replaced,—
At least, until another year!

Love's Day

O that my heart were the rose of the garden
Love is the Lord of, and Summer the Warden,
Where you would come for the cool of the air,
With eyes full of pleading, with lips full of pardon,
And take me and break me and scatter me there,
Raining in rose leaves, ruined away,
Where none can know of and none can say,
And my heart, my heart, should have had its day.

O that my heart were the breezes that sigh for you
Over the passionate flowers that die for you,
Beating against your window at night—
O like a flame I would quiver and fly for you,
Fast to your dream, as you lay there white,
Lost in the moonlight, wafted away,
Where none can know of and none can say,
And my heart, my heart, should have had its day.

O my poor heart, and where can I throw it?
Love as I love—'twere a sin to show it,
For years have changed and the hour gone by—
My heart must break, you must never know it;
The love I love can but dream and die,
Weeping by night and wasting by day,
Where none can know of, and none can say,
And my heart, my heart, shall have had its day.

GARDEN-PERIL

Over a garden paling
In a soft midsummer day
A butterfly went sailing,
Went he, as who should say,
"There's nought in this world ailing,
So let the world be gay."

Went he from pink to posy,
But had no mind to sip,
The blossoms all were rosy,
With dew upon their lip;
So snug felt he and cosy,
The whole parterre would skip.

So often had it flaunted,
The scent was growing stale;
The same old roses panted,
The same old lilies pale
Their honey-flavor vaunted,—
The summer's tedious tale.

Heart-whole, the jaunty sailor
Cruised, all his canvas set,
Deigned not a rose to hail, or
In one his thirst to wet;
No bud shall be his jailer,
No coy cup make him fret.

Ha! up his colors flaring
He nailed them to the mast,
And down the garden bearing,
His reef he found at last:
Too late, too late for wearing,
Too late the lead to cast.

So sudden, so secluded,
So mantled in a mist,
Her violet-temper brooded,
Not waiting to be kissed,
But not to be eluded:—
His wreck became a tryst!

A Woman's Death Wound

It left upon her tender flesh no trace.
The murderer is safe. As swift as light
The weapon fell, and, in the summer night,
Did scarce the silent dewy air displace.
'Twas but a word. A blow had been less base.
Like dumb beast branded by an iron white
With heat, she turned in blind and helpless flight,
But then remembered, and with piteous face
Came back.

    Since then, the world has nothing missed
In her in voice or smile. But she—each day
She counts until her dying be complete.
One moan she makes, and ever doth repeat,
"Oh lips which I had loved and kissed and kissed,
Did I deserve to die this bitterest way?"

A Lover's Tests

I sat today beneath the pine
    And saw the long lake shine.
The wind was weary, and the day
    Sank languidly away
Behind the forest's purple rim:
The sun was fair for me, I lived for him!

I did not miss you. All was sweet,
    Sky, earth, and soul complete
In harmony, which could afford
    No more, nor spoil the chord.
Could I be blest, and you afar,
Were other I, or you, than what we are?

The sifted silver of the night
    Rained down a strange delight;
The moon's moist beam on meadows made
    Pale bars athwart the shade,
And murmurs crept from tree to tree,
Mysterious whispers—not from you to me!

I stirred the embers, roused the brand
    And mused: on either hand
The pedigree of human thought
    Sang, censured, cheered, or taught.
Pausing at each Titanic line,
I caught no echo from your soul to mine!

And last, when life recast its form
    To passive rest and warm,
Ere the soft, lingering senses cease
    In sleep's half-conscious peace,
The wish I might have fashioned died
In dreams that never brought you to my side!

Farewell! my nature's highest stress
    Mine equal shall possess.
'Tis easier to renounce, or wait,
    Haply, the perfect fate.
My coldness is the haughty fire
That naught consumes except its full desire!

Her Word of Reproach

We must not quarrel, whatever we do;
    For if I was (but I was not!) wrong,
    Here are the tears for it, here are the tears:—
What else has a woman to offer you?
    Love might not last for a thousand years,
You know, though the stars should rise so long.

Oh you, you talk in a man's great way!—
    So, love would last though the stars should fall?
Why, yes. If it last to the grave, indeed,
    After the grave last on it may.
But—in the grave? Will its dust take heed
    Of anything sweet—or the sweetest of all?

Ah, death is nothing! It may be so.
    Yet, granting at least that death is death,
(Pray look at the rose, and hear the bird,)
    Whatever it is—we must die to know!
Sometime we may long to say one word
    Together—and find we have no breath.

Ah me, how divine you are growing again!—
    How coldly sure that the Heavens are sure,
Whither too lightly you always fly
    To hide from the passion of human pain.
Come, grieve that the Earth is not secure,
    For this one night—and forget the sky!

Forgiven

Today I must forgive you in a song,
    And put all from me for the old love's sake,—
Leave the vexed question, who was right or wrong,
    When love broke up, and our hearts did not break;
And think of you as one not far away.
What is there floating in the air today
    That gets old, sleeping memories awake?

A lark began it, singing out of sight;
    Then, from wet woods, a thrush put in your name,
And sang it over for my heart's delight;
    And with the wet blown breath of flowers there came
A tender, subtle fragrance of regret:
On dead love's grave the grass grows greener yet,
    And you, today, far-off, may think the same.

I have a fancy we go out today,
    And tread the woods together, and again
Go, both of us, the dear, familiar way.
    Soft hazy light succeeds to quiet rain,
And thrushes, whose low chant you understand,
With songs of blackbirds reach us, on each hand,—
    Nature is for us, in our joy and pain.

Let us remember how, in days gone by
    When our lives mixed together for love's sake,
We stood thus, while the light went out on high
    And birds stopped singing; while from field and brake,
Whence bats flew out in stealthy, circling flight,
We heard the small, sweet voices of the night
    Begin in faltering music to awake.

You thought me so much better than I was—
    I found you perfect—Ah, to blame, to blame!
The sweet hallucination could but pass,
    And with the passing how much sharpness came!

You, nothing perfect—cold, intolerant,
With mind on some far, shadowy good intent—
    Your love a moonbeam; mine the sun's large flame.

Well, what is left for us to say or do?
    So many thorns you found in my poor rose
I took it from your hand, and laughed at you;
    The tears came after—then came bland repose—
Almost forgetfulness—until, today,
The thrushes singing of you all the way
    Found me the song my wanderings to close.

I deemed you should be with me, but, alas!
    That sweetest thought could not my fancy hold:
I only trail my shadow on the grass—
    Here's nature to myself, and rest untold—
Yet the time wants you, and the peaceful place
Would be more peaceful for your peaceful face,
    Your gracious figure, and your hair's red gold.

Ah! woods and fields all speak to me of you,
    As you, in town, would speak of these to me:
Gray, quiet air faint sunlight falters through,
    The rest of hills, the eve's tranquillity
Through which some late, last bird flies home and sings—
We love you for your semblance to these things,
    But find behind no fair reality.

And is this the forgiveness that I planned?
    And do I chide you to the end? Nay, Sweet!
So long ago since we loosed hand from hand,
    My love and sorrow both have been complete,
And both have almost faded out of sight,—
Almost I say, you understand, not quite—
    Your voice might quicken still my pulse's beat.

It seems a strange forgiveness—yet, indeed,
    You are forgiven, for the thrushes' sake—
Live on and prosper! We have no more need

Of one another—no more thirsts to slake—
And many days I find, and many miss,
But haply nevermore a day like this,
    To kiss old sleeping memories awake.

We Twain

I

Oh, Earth and Heaven are far apart!
    But what if they were one,
And neither you nor I, Sweetheart,
    Had anyway misdone?
When we, like laughing rivers fleet,
    That cannot choose but flow,
Among the flowers should meet and greet,
    Should meet and mingle so,
        Sweetheart,—
    That would be sweet, I know.

II

No need to swerve and drift apart,
    Or any bliss resign;
Then I should all be yours, Sweetheart,
    And you would all be mine.
But ah, to rush, defiled and brown,
    From thaw of smirchèd snow,
To spoil the corn, beat down and drown
    The rath, red lilies low—
        Sweetheart,
    I do not want you so!

III

For you and I are far apart;
    And never may we meet,
Till you are glad and grand, Sweetheart,
    Till I am fair and sweet.
Till morning-light has kissed us white
    As highest Alpine snow,
Till both are brave and bright of sight,—
    Go wander high or low,

Sweetheart:
    For God will have it so.

IV

Oh, Heaven and Earth are far apart!
    If you are bond or free,
And if you climb or crawl, Sweetheart,
    Can no way hinder me.
But see you come in lordly state,
    With mountain winds a-glow,
When I, by dazzling gate shall wait,
    To meet and love you so,
        Sweetheart!
    That will be Heaven, I know.

A Fallen House

The End has come, which never seems the End,
    And thou and I, who loved so long and well,
    Find, at the last, our Fate implacable—
Stern Fate, who wills not that our lives should blend
But overthrows fair things we did intend:
    The house in which long time we thought to dwell
    Was built above a ruin, so it fell—
Great was the fall, which no man could defend.

Behold it lies there overthrown, that house—
In its fair halls no comer shall carouse—
    Its broad rooms with strange Silences are filled;
No fire upon its crumbling hearth shall glow,
Seeing its desolation men shall know
    On ruin of what was they may not build.

The Wanderer

Love comes back to his vacant dwelling,—
 The old, old Love that we knew of yore!
 We see him stand by the open door,
With his great eyes sad, and his bosom swelling.

He makes as though in our arms repelling,
 He fain would lie as he lay before;—
Love comes back to his vacant dwelling,—
 The old, old Love that we knew of yore!

Ah, who shall help us from over-spelling
 That sweet forgotten, forbidden lore!
 E'en as we doubt in our heart once more,
With a rush of tears to our eyelids welling,
Love comes back to his vacant dwelling.

At Twilight

At twilight, when the air is very still,
When the last daylight cleaves to the last hill,
And streams give answer to the changing sky,
When we go home together, Grief and I,
And gaze again from the old window-sill,—

Then is my life most desolate; until
Your Angel, giving answer to my will,
Troubles the sullen pools of memory
      At twilight.

All yours, O Love, are those sweet thoughts that fill
My heart as brim high as the sacred rill
The sad eye'd throng looked on so longingly.
There I am healed. There, as the years go by,
My love for you rises more chastened still
      At twilight.

THE MARSHES OF GLYNN

Glooms of the live-oaks, beautiful-braided and woven
With intricate shades of the vines that myriad-cloven
    Clamber the forks of the multiform boughs,—
        Emerald twilights,—
        Virginal shy lights,
Wrought of the leaves to allure to the whisper of vows,
When lovers pace timidly down through the green colonnades
    Of the dim sweet woods, of the dear dark woods,
        Of the heavenly woods and glades,
That run to the radiant marginal sand-beach within
        The wide sea-marshes of Glynn;—

Beautiful glooms, soft dusks in the noon-day fire,—
Wildwood privacies, closets of lone desire,
Chamber from chamber parted with wavering arras of leaves,—
Cells for the passionate pleasure of prayer to the soul that grieves,
Pure with a sense of the passing of saints through the wood,
Cool for the dutiful weighing of ill with good;—

O braided dusks of the oak and woven shades of the vine,
While the riotous noon-day sun of the June-day long did shine,
Ye held me fast in your heart and I held you fast in mine;
But now when the noon is no more, and riot is rest,
And the sun doth wait at the ponderous gate of the West,
And the slant yellow beam down the wood-aisle doth seem
Like a lane into heaven that leads from a dream,—
Ay, now, when my soul all day hath drunken the soul of the oak,
And my heart is at ease from men, and the wearisome sound of the
    stroke
    Of the scythe of time and the trowel of trade is low,
    And belief overmasters doubt, and I know that I know,
    And my spirit is grown to a lordly great compass within,
    That the length and the breadth and the sweep of the marshes of
        Glynn
    Will work me no fear like the fear they have wrought me of yore
    When length was fatigue, and when breadth was but bitterness sore,

And when terror and shrinking and dreary unnamable pain
Drew over me out of the merciless width of the plain,—

    Oh, now, unafraid, I am fain to face
        The vast sweet visage of space.
    To the edge of the wood I am drawn, I am drawn,
Where the gray beach glimmering runs, as a belt of the dawn,
        For a mete and a mark
          To the forest-dark:—
            So:
    Affable live-oak, bending low—
      Thus—with your favor—soft, with a reverent hand,
    (Not lightly touching your person, Lord of the land!)
    Swinging your beauty aside, with a step I stand
        On the firm-packed sand,
        Free
    By a world of marsh that borders a world of sea.
    Sinuous southward and sinuous northward the shimmering
      band
    Of the sand-beach fastens the fringe of the marsh to the folds of
      the land.
Inward and outward to northward and southward the beach-lines
    linger and curl
As a silver-wrought garment that clings to and follows the firm sweet
    limbs of a girl.
    Vanishing, swerving, evermore curving again into sight,
    Softly the sand-beach wavers away to a dim gray looping of light.
    And what if behind me to westward the wall of the woods stands
      high?
    The world lies east: how ample, the marsh and the sea and the sky!
    A league and a league of marsh-grass, waist-high, broad in the
      blade,
    Green, and all of a height, and unflecked with a light or a shade,
      Stretch leisurely off, in a pleasant plain,
      To the terminal blue of the main.

Oh, what is abroad in the marsh and the terminal sea?
    Somehow my soul seems suddenly free
    From the weighing of fate and the sad discussion of sin,

By the length and the breadth and the sweep of the marshes of Glynn.

Ye marshes, how candid and simple and nothing-with-holding and free
Ye publish yourselves to the sky and offer yourselves to the sea!

Tolerant plains, that suffer the sea and the rains and the sun,
Ye spread and span like the catholic man who hath mightily won
God out of knowledge and good out of infinite pain
And sight out of blindness and purity out of a stain.

As the marsh-hen secretly builds on the watery sod,
Behold I will build me a nest on the favor of God:
I will fly in the favor of God as the marsh-hen flies
In the freedom that fills all the space 'twixt the marsh and the skies:
By so many roots as the marsh-grass sends in the sod
I will heartily lay me a hold on the favor of God.

Oh, like to the favor of God, for the largeness within,
Is the range of the marshes, the liberal marshes of Glynn.

And the sea lends large, as the marsh: lo, out of his plenty the sea
Pours fast: full soon the time of the flood of the tide must be:
    Look how the grace of the sea doth go
    About and about through the intricate channels that flow
        Here and there,
            Everywhere,
Till his waters have flooded the uttermost creeks and the high-lying
    lanes,
    And the marsh is meshed with a million veins,
    That like as with rosy and silvery essences flow
        In the rose-and-silver evening glow.
            Farewell, my lord Sun!
        The creeks overflow: a thousand rivulets run
'Twixt the roots of the sod; the blades of the marsh-grass stir;
Passeth a hurrying sound of wings that nestward whirr:
Passeth, and all is still: and the currents cease to run;
    And the sea and the marsh are one.
        How still the plains of the waters be!
            The tide is in his ecstasy.

The tide is at his highest height:
      And it is night.

And now from the vast of the Lord will the waters of sleep
    Roll in on the souls of men,
    But who will reveal to our waking ken
The forms that swim and the shapes that creep
      Under the waters of sleep?
And I would I could know what swimmeth below when the tide
    comes in
On the length and the breadth of the marvellous marshes of Glynn.

Ballad of the Wicked Nephew

It was a wicked Nephew bold
Who uprose in the night,
And ground upon a huge grindstone
His penknife, sharp and bright.

And while the sparks were flying wild
The cellar floor upon,
Quoth he unto himself, "I will
Despatch my Uncle John!

"His property is large, and if
He dies, and leaves a Will,
His loving Nephew (that's myself)
Won't get a dollar bill.

"I'll hie unto my Uncle's bed,
His chamber well I know,
And there I'll find his pocket-book
Safe under his pil-*low*.

"With this bright steel I'll slay him first,
Because that is the way
They do such things, I understand,
In Boucicault's new Play."

By this the anxious moon retired,
(For all the stars were in),—
"'Tis very dark," the Nephew cried,
"But I can find my kin!"

"Come forth my trusty weapon now!"
(Or words to that effect),
He shouted to his little blade—
Whose power he did suspect.

Then out he starts. His Uncle's door
Is thirteen doors from his:—
He gains the latch, which upward flies,
And straight inside he is!

One pause upon the entry stair,
And one upon the mat,—
How still the house at such an hour!
How mewless lies the cat!

"O Nephew! Nephew! be not rash,
Turn back, and then 'turn in';
Your Uncle still is sound asleep,
And you devoid of sin!

"The gallows-tree was never built
For handsome lads like you,—
Get thee to bed! (as kind Macbeth
Wished *his* young man to do)."

He will not be advised,—he stands
Beside the sleeping form,—
The hail begins to beat outside
A tattoo for the storm.

"'Tis not too late—repent! repent!
And all may yet be well!"
"Repent yourself!" the Nephew sneers—
And at it goes pell-mell!

To right and left he carves his way,—
At least thus did it seem,—
And, after he had done the deed,
Woke up from his bad dream.

And swift to Uncle John he ran,
When daylight climbed the hill,
And told him all—and Uncle John
Put Nephew in his Will.

The Angler

An angler by a brook doth lie;
Upon his hook, a painted fly;
A dream's soft shadow in his eye.
Thus, like a charmèd prince he seems,
Destined a glorious prize to win,
Which, like a jewelled javelin,
Poised, as in air, on quivering fin
Before his vision gleams.

With purest blue, the blissful sky
Pavilions him right royally.
Sometimes an oriole flames on high;
A bee, impetuous, sparkles by;
A bobolink, ecstatic, flings
Bubbles of music down the air;
And so he gathers everywhere
From realms of ease, all joys most rare,
Like pearls on silken strings.

The Rebel Flower

Across the garden paths she led
Her Tory guest, with stately tread;
A Boston beauty in her prime,
With courage equal to the time
That tried men's souls, her loyal heart
Cried out against the craven part
It was her irksome fate to play
As courteous hostess on that day.

A gracious, gallant air he wore,
A gracious, gallant rank he bore,
This Tory guest, yet well she knew
Beneath the air, the rank, perdue,
A crafty treacherous purpose hid,
As poisons lurked beneath the lid
Of jewelled caskets long ago,
When every friend might prove a foe.

The garden beds were gay with bloom,—
Fair treasures which have given room
Long since at Fashion's stern decree
To splendors from across the sea.
For close beside the stately rose,
No tyranny can e'er depose,
The sturdy camomile did lift
Its myriad blossoms' snowy drift.

"What flower is this?" The Tory guest
Half paused to ask in idle quest.
A moment's thought, then sweet and clear,
"The Rebel flower, we call it here,"
She answered him, this Boston dame
Of lovely mien and rebel fame.
"How's this?" he laughed; and laughing sent
A keen look at the fair face bent

In modest musing on the flower
She'd newly named within that hour.
"How's this, sweet dame, and why, pray tell,
So fair a flower a name so fell
Should win and wear?" A swift smile sped
Across her face, then slow she said,
"Because, my lord, this flower that's won
Your meed of praise, when trampled on,

Springs from the dust and thrives anew
In fresher vigor than it knew
Before such blows of fortune came,—
Thus rightly winning name and fame."
"Ah, ha!" laughed out the Tory guest
At this bold speech, "a pretty jest
I' faith, sweet dame, and bravely said.
When next we meet, perhaps a tread

Of weightier heels may have crushed out
These boasted claims, and put to rout
Your rebel flowers till name and fame
Are lost beneath the dust of shame."
She laughed him back, with laughter born
Of gay disdain and sparkling scorn.—
"When next, we meet, my lord," she said,
"This rebel flower will lift its head

In lustier vigor than before,
And name and fame for evermore
Shall flourish bravely in the land
Despite th' oppressors' heel or hand!"
When next they met, my lord had laid
His sword beneath the rebel blade,
And she who prophesied the fate
Of British valor, stood in state
On British soil, an honored guest,
Wearing upon her lovely breast,
In smiling triumph for that hour,
A posy called "The Rebel Flower!"

The Bride of War

(Arnold's March to Canada, 1775)

I

The trumpet with a giant sound
     Its harsh war-summons wildly sings;
     And, bursting forth like mountain springs,
Poured from the hillside camping-ground,
   Each swift battalion shouting flings
Its force into line. Then you may see
The men, broad-shouldered, heavily
Sway to the swing of the march, their heads
Dark like the stones in river-beds.

   Lightly the autumn breezes
   Play with the shining dust-cloud
   Rising to the sunset rays
   From feet of the moving column.
   Soft, as you listen, comes
   The echo of iterant drums,

Brought by the breezes light
From the files that follow the road.
A moment their guns have glowed
Sun-smitten; then out of sight
They suddenly sink,
Like men who touch a new grave's brink!

II

So it was the march began,
   The march of Morgan's riflemen,
Who like iron held the van
In unhappy Arnold's plan
   To win Wolfe's daring fame again.

With them, by her husband's side,
 Jemima Warner, nobly free,
Moved more fair than when, a bride,
One year since she strove to hide
 The blush it was a joy to see.

Strangely sounds this name of woman,
 Crude and cold,—Jemima Warner;
Yet the shrill-blown trumpets summon
 Her to lead this antique story:—

 Not in guise of hero-mourner,
 Nor as one who loved a foeman,
 But a dauntless peril-scorner
 Whose calm strength was more than glory.

III

O distant, terrible forests of Maine,
With huge trees numberless as the rain
 That striketh your lonely lakes!
(It strikes and sings through the years, but wakes
No answering echo of joy or pain.)

Your tangled wilderness was tracked
By the doers of many a treacherous act,—
 Puritan, pagan, and priest:
Where wolf and panther and serpent ceased,
Man added the horrors your dark maze lacked.

Like the fretting of worms on withered wood,
The land was scarred with deeds not good.
 What if its venomous spell
Breathed into Arnold a prompting of Hell,
With slow empoisoning force indued?

As through that dreary realm he went,
Followed a shape of dark portent:

Pard-like, of furtive eye, with brain
To treason narrowing, Aaron Burr
Moved loyal-seeming in the train
Led by the arch-conspirator.
And craven Enos[1] closed the rear,
Whose honor's flame died out in fear.
Not sooner does the dry bough burn
And into fruitless ashes turn,
Than he with whispered, false command
Flung back the hundreds in his hand,
Fled like a shade, and all forsook.
Wherever Arnold bent his look
Danger and doubt around him hung;
And pale Disaster, shrouded, flung
Black omens in his track, as though
The fingers of a future woe
Already clutched his life, to wring
Some expiation for the thing
That he was yet to do. A chill
Struck helpless many a steadfast will
Within the ranks; the very air
Rang with a thunder-toned despair;
And round them, lost in drifts of snow,
The hills like blind guides seemed to go!

IV

Yet still devout, through loss and doubt,
    One woman's loyal heart—whose pain
Filled it with white celestial light—
Shone starry-constant like the North,
    And sacred like a fane.
But he whose ring Jemima wore,
By want and weariness all unstrung,
Though strong and honest of heart and young,

---

1. Colonel Enos, of Connecticut, commanded the rear guard, consisting of eight hundred men, in this terrible march, and deserted his chief, with the whole force confided to him, while the expedition was struggling through the wilderness in the Dead River region.

Shrank at the blast that pierced so frore—
Like a huge, invisible bird of prey
Furious launch'd from Labrador
And the granite cliffs of Saguenay!
Along the bleak Dead River's banks
They forced amain their frozen way;
But ever from the thinning ranks
Shapes of ice would reel and fall,
Human shapes, whose dying prayer
Floated, a mute white mist, in air;—
The crowding snow their pall.
Spectre-like, Famine drew near:
Her doom-word hummed in his ear,
And the sounds of life grew fewer
As she drew him closer to her.
Ah, weak were woman's hands to reach
And save him from the hellish charms
And wizard motion of those arms!
Yet only noble womanhood
The wife her dauntless part could teach:
She shared with him the last dry food
And thronged with hopefulness her speech,—
As when hard by her home the flood
Of rushing Conestoga fills
Its depth afresh from springtide rills!

All, all in vain!
For far behind the invading rout
    These two were left alone;
And in the waste their wildest shout
    Seemed but a smothered groan.
Like sheeted wanderers from the grave
They moved, and yet seemed not to stir,
As icy gorge and sere-leaf'd grove
Of withered oak and shrouded fir
Were passed and onward still they strove,
While the loud wind's artillery clave

The air, and furious sleety rain
Swung like a sword above the plain!

V

They crossed the hills; they came to where
Through an arid gloom the river Chaudière
Fled like a Maenad with outstreaming hair;
And there the soldier sank, and died.

Death-dumb he fell, yet ere life sped,
Child-like on her knee he laid his head.
She strove to pray; but all words fled
Save those their love had sanctified.

And then her voice rose waveringly
To the notes of a mother's lullaby;
But her song was only "Ah, must thou die!"
And to her his eyes death-still replied.

VI

Dead leaves and stricken boughs
She heaped o'er the fallen form:

Wolf nor hawk nor lawless storm
Him from his rest should rouse:
But first, with solemn vows,
Took rifle, pouch, and horn,
And the belt that he had worn.
For, widowed and unhappy evermore,
She gave herself to be the bride of war.
Then, onward pressing fast
Through the forest rude and vast
Hunger-wasted, fever-parch'd—
Many bitter days she marched
With bleeding feet that spurned the flinty pain;

One thought always throbbing through her brain:
"They shall never say, *He was afraid,*—
They shall never cry, *The coward stayed!*"

Now the wilderness is passed;
Now the first hut reached, at last.

Ho, dwellers by the frontier trail,
Come forth and greet the bride of war!
From cabin and from settlement
They come to speed her on her way:—
Maidens, whose ruddy cheeks grow pale

With pity never felt before;
Children that cluster at the door;
Mothers, whose toil-worn hands are lent
To help, or bid her longer stay.
But through them all she passes on,
Strangely martial, fair and wan;
Nor waits to listen to their cheers
That sound so faintly in her ears.
For now all scenes around her shift
Like those before a racer's eyes
When, foremost sped and madly swift,
Forth stretching toward the goal he flies,
Yet feels his strength wane with his breath
And purpose fail 'mid fears of death;—
Till, like the flashing of a lamp,
Starts forth the sight of Arnold's camp.

Then to the leader she is brought—
The man who wronged his country's trust—
And speaks her grandly loyal thought
That should have bowed him in the dust:
"Your rifle-bearer on the way
Perished, but I come to say
His faith is kept with you today!"

Herald of the brave in story,
    Let the poet proudly summon
Honor for Jemima Warner,
For the fearless peril-scorner;
    Honor for the high-souled woman
Whose calm strength was more than glory!

From Herzegovina

There were some forty men of us, strong men and young together,
Went marching up the mountain-side that glorious August weather;
All four by four and step by step, with carabine to shoulder,
And girt with glittering yatagans—Ho! never a band was bolder!
Our blood-red tassels switched our ears, blood-stained our white
    apparel;
We feasted on the wild goats' flesh, and drank strong wine by barrel;
And flushed it forth like fire, and sang and shouted out in chorus,
And swore by all God's sacraments, holding his cross before us,
Each one that he was Freedom's son and everyone a brother,
And each to the sun discharged his gun and manlike kiss'd the other;
And hand to hand, and breast to breast, that glorious August weather,
We swore to hunt the Turk and feast and drink and die together.

For forty days and forty nights we rattled on like thunder,
And shot the damnèd Turk dogs down—no man of us fell under!
For forty days and forty nights with long moustaches flying,
We hurled the Turk from crag to crag—no Christian dreamed of
    dying!
For forty days the vines and maize were blazing with our fire,
And four by four and step by step we strode on higher and higher.
One day we came on a chestnut grove and chose it out for nooning,
Our heads were wreathed up from the sun as if we came from pruning;
Cool strawberry plants grew all about; bright blue, between the
    branches,
You could not say which was blue bay or blue sky where it blanches;
For everywhere were simmering air and slumbering slopes of heather;
And farther away one reek yet lay and a white sail faint as a feather.

We stretched our bare limbs in the moss, our hot things on the
    thickets,
And all was still on shore and hill, except the ceaseless crickets,
No bird was heard and no leaf stirr'd and no one dreamed of
    battle,—
When quick a white flame quivered past, the jays whirled out, and a
    rattle

                GEORGE PARSONS LATHROP

Of bullets crackled against the twigs, and, snatching our guns in
     wonder,
We found our youngest clawing the ground, his left lung shot asunder.
For forty days and forty nights each man was like a mother;
We made a litter of tender boughs, each one relieved the other;
We gave him all we had, and hard we fought our way and bore him
Both night and day the slippery way, though nothing could restore
     him.
He lay like lead upon our hearts, like dead upon our shoulder,
His joints were rotting in the thews and no corpse could be colder.
At last one murmured:—"'Tis no use. The Turks are pressing faster,—
We had better slay him from his pain than wait a worse disaster."
It must have been his heart that heard. God knows! He muttered:
     "Hear me.

     "My comrades, I've no fear of Death, 'tis death who seems to fear
          me!
So take me to the highest ground where grows the golden heather,
The wind and light are brighter there than all one's life together.
And let me die there as God wills and leave me where you lay me,
And may my dead curse doubly strike whoever dares gainsay me!
And further yet I pray of you, even to the last brother
The Turks may spare, that you shall bear no tidings to my mother.
She stands her distaff in her hands among them at the fountain,
And sighs that old sad sigh of hers, and looks up at the mountain.
Above them shakes the mulberry-tree I have climbed with many a
     fellow;
About the top I've cut my name—the leaves must now be yellow.
She must not know how matters go; her poor old hands are hoary;
It can't be long, so let her die still dreaming of my glory.
And bid her work the white stuff done she has spun against I marry;
And say I've joined the Servian men, and say she must not tarry."

Running the Blockade

A Chase in Soundings

Hilloa-Hoa! the falcon and swallow,
Yo-hoicks the fox and the hound;
As if you could hear the long, four-footed, hollow
Reverberate beat on the ground,
And feel yourself swing in the saddle,
At the fore-shoulder's reach in the straddle,
As the hunter comes up to the bound.

Hove in the stays, she lay,
In the blockading grounds,
Of the North Carolina sounds,
Beleaguered half a day,
The good ship Heir of Lynn:
The still air shut her in
The very focus of light;
Where the sea grows hot and white,
As if it had turned to salt
Or solid rock, with a fault
That clipped the horizon's edge
In a long, irregular ledge.

In the summer of '63,
As still as they could be
The sea and air; and every
Spar lost in a reverie
Over its shadow, under
The sea, in curious wonder.
Not a cat's-paw turned the streamer,
To spell at it letter by letter;
And for fifty leagues and better,
You could see the smoke of a steamer
Drifting down in the offing.

You could hear the sullen coughing,
Over sixty miles away,
At Wilmington harbor and bay,—
The pounding of cannon and mortar,
And the groan of torpedoes under
The sea, that came over her quarter,
Like the bellow of smothered thunder.
Uneasily looked the master
Now at the sea, and then
Off in a dream again
Of home, as the boa's'in cast her
Dipsy[1] lead in the shallow,
To a sort of nasal tune,
Larded with talk and tallow,
In the bight of the afternoon;
Drawling from sea-worn topics,
To sudden squalls in the tropics;
And lee shores whose hot lips
Had opened and swallowed ships,—
Till the slow talk seemed to pool
In the old Annapolis school;
And the master was "Joe" again,
With his messmate, Geordie of Maine,
Who loved, with loves like his own,
Sweethearts they never had won—
Like the small blue flowers that live but a day,
Sweet things, in the inlets of Chesapeake bay.

The skies got bluer and bluer,
Till the far-off gunboat knew her,
And came up, hand over hand,
With a rushing, like falling sand,
Of the coils of her screw propeller,
Like the rifles that twist out her shell, or
The leverage fold and grapple
Of the sinewy boa-constrictor,

---

1. Deep-sea.

While her stem peeled the scum as an apple,
And the plunge of her steam beat the drums of a victor.

But, like omens in viscera,
Old Romans sought for;
As the stars fought with Sisera,—
Faster and faster,
And over and past her,
Swirled the cone of the cyclone and fought her.

It touched the sails of the schooner,
The turn of a sandglass sooner;
And, breaking in sudden bloom,—
From her foretop studding-sail,
Aft to her spanker-boom,
Down to her channel rail,

Fore to her flying jibs;—
Like a lily when it buds
She flowers out of her ribs,
White as the salt-sea seeds;
Bobbing about, like a cup.
Then a shout, and the hunt is up.

Hilloa-hoa! the falcon and swallow,
Yo-hoicks! the fox and the hound;
As if you could hear the long, four-footed, hollow
Reverberate beat of the ground,
And feel yourself swing in the saddle,
At the fore-shoulder's reach in the straddle,
As the hunter comes up to the bound.

"A lee shore and a squall!
There's but one of them all,"
As he steamed within hail,
Said the Gunboat commander,
"Of all that I know,
That would dare carry sail

To beach her and land her,—
Annapolis Joe."

As swivels of hail
Beat tattoo on the sail,
And he looked on the sea,
Where tempests unchain
Reefs hid in white rain;
"You'll want boots to follow me
All night," said the master,
"With your wrought-iron roster,
Old Geordie of Maine."

Ship ahoy! Heave to!
The wind seemed to wrestle
With steam in the vessel,
Elastic and pliant,
And wrench the propeller
With the strength of a giant,
As if to compel her
To shrink from the danger,
Her keel timbers ran on:
But grimly defiant,
And louder and louder,
In the bursting of powder,
Spoke the lips of her cannon.

Hilloa-hoa! the falcon and swallow,
Yo-hoicks! the fox and the hound;
As if you could hear the long, four-footed, hollow
Reverberate beat on the ground,
And feel yourself swing in the saddle,
At the fore-shoulder's reach in the straddle,
As the hunter comes up to the bound.

"It's Joe to be sure,"
Said the naval commander,
"And he's got a king's ransom of stores in his keel;
I'll sink her or land her

Rawbones on a leeshore,
To feed the Sound fishes on his powder and steel."

A reef rose between,
Where the keel of the sea seemed to jib and careen,
And pitch on its beam ends,
About which the water ran smooth with vehemence,
Like the gates of a lock when its hinges are swung,
And the bore of the current shoots out in a tongue.
But, taut and close-lasted,
From keelson to mast head;

Spanker vangs to sprit-sail-yards,
And flying jib-boom,
As true to her halyards
As belle of the room
When her feet, to the click of the castanets clipping,
Make rhymes to the music's adagios tripping,—
As dangerously quick as Herodias' daughter,—
While the wind kissed her lacings and whipped round her quarter,
And pitch-piped its bagpipes as shrill as a demon,
The sloop felt her tiller;
Double banked her propeller;
And rushed at the sluice with a full head of steam on.

Hilloa-hoa! the falcon and swallow,
Yo-hoicks! the fox and the hound;
As if you could hear the long, four-footed, hollow
Reverberate beat on the ground,
And feel yourself swing in the saddle,
At the fore-shoulder's reach in the straddle,
As the hunter comes up to the bound.

But the fugitive ship,
Like a wild thing at bay,
That will double and slip
From corner to panel,
Like a fox, stole away.
The nips of the channel,

GEORGE PARSONS LATHROP

In shoulder and knee,
Seemed to rise and bend over her;
The bellowing sea,
To open and cover her;
And where the surf plunges
Through coral and sponges
In slings of the wind as light as a feather,
To rove the blue phosphorus frost in her shrouds,
The burst of the clouds,
Mixed the sea and the sand and the sky altogether,
And the welkin cracked open with terrible brightening,
Till the bed of the sea seemed to bristle with lightning;
And over, and under
The clamor of waves, pealed the toll of the thunder.

> *Hilloa-hoa! the falcon and swallow,*
> *Yo-hoicks! the fox and the hound;*
> *As if you could hear the long, four-footed, hollow*
> *Reverberate beat on the ground,*
> *And feel yourself swing in the saddle,*
> *At the fore-shoulder's reach in the straddle,*
> *As the hunter comes up to the bound.*

So, all through the night, in the darkness they grope.
In the wash of the water, and swish of the spray,
Clung the sloop to the chase, as if towed by a rope,
Till the morning gun slipped it, at breaking of day.
Tira la, sang the bugles,—a fox stole away!
Stole away; stole away: stole away; stole away:
Tira la sang the bugles—a fox stole away.

In Wilmington town, there's a ringing of bells
As the people go down, to see her come in,
With her flag at the forepeak, as everyone tells
Of the old ballad luck of the ship HEIR OF LYNN.

If you ever meet Josey, or Geordie of Maine,
You will run the chase over in soundings again.

THE RHONE CRADLE

(A Vignette of Travel)

This is the fair bed of the infant Rhone,
A cradle broad with fruits and sunshine strown,
A dreamy valley guarded by tall shapes
They call the Alps; where miles of clustering grapes,
Purple of eye, in leafy garments green
Load down the hills, that near and nearer lean
To watch the rushing river and the small
Traffic of men close under that scarred wall
Of some free-booting baron's ancient tower.
Gone are the baron and his murderous power,
And like some uncouth beast of earliest time
The gray bones of the ruined castle climb
The steep, yet utterly inert remain,—
A fossil record, which the years disdain
To wipe away. Here once the Cæsar bore
His Roman eagle above the icy roar
Of mountain-torrents.
                    Many centuries passed;
But Gaul sent forth *her* eagle, at the last:
Napoleon's iron hand cut out a path
Across the rocky Simplon; poured his wrath
From out the clouds; and where the deep gorge breaks
Through caverned gloom, to reach the Lombard lakes,
His legions swept to Italy, to Rome,—
The conqueror's goal, the world-subduer's home.

Lo, whatsoe'er befall or tribe or town,
The growing river still flows broadening down,
Not otherwise than when it first began;
Still young, still wild, though many a white-hair'd man
Hath laid him down beside its foamy bank,
Nor ever risen again from where he sank.
Child Rhone, thy course is marked by death and woe:
Wilt thou thus swift and laughing always go?

GEORGE PARSONS LATHROP

JOHN CARMAN

John Carman of Carmantown
    Worked hard through the longest day;
He drove his awl and he snapped his thread,
    And he had but little to say.

He had but little to say
    Except to a neighbor's child:
Three summers old she was, and her eyes
    Had a look that was deep and wild.

Her hair was heavy and brown,
    Like clouds in a starry night.
She came and sat by the cobbler's bench,
    And his soul was filled with delight.

No kith nor kin had he,
    And he never went gadding about;
A strange, shy man, the people said,
    And they could not make him out.

And some of them shook their heads,
    And wouldn't tell what they'd heard.
But he drove his awl and snapped his thread,—
    And he always kept his word.

And the little child that knew him
    Better than all the rest,
She threw her arms around his neck
    And went to sleep on his breast.

One day in that dreadful summer
    When children died by the score,
John Carman glanced from his work and saw
    Her mother there at the door.

He knew by the look in her face,—
    And his own on a sudden turned white.
He rose from his bench and followed her out,
    And watched by the child that night.

He tended her day and night;
    He watched by her night and day:
He saw the cruel pain in her eyes;
    He saw her lips turn gray.

*   *   *   *   *   *

The day that the child was buried,
    John Carman went back to his last;
And the neighbors said that for weeks and weeks
    Not a word his clenched lips passed.

"He takes it hard," they gossiped.
    "Poor man, he's lacking in wit."—
"I'll drop in, today," said Deacon Gray,
    "And comfort him up a bit."

So Deacon Gray dropped in
    With a kind and neighborly air;
And before he left, he kneeled on the floor,
    And wrestled with God in prayer.

And he said: "O Lord, thou hast stricken
    This child in its babyhood:
In Thy own way, we beseech and pray,
    Bring forth from evil good."

That night the fire-bells rang,
    And the flames shot up to the sky,
And into the street, as pale as a sheet,
    The town-folk flock and cry.

The bells ring loud and long;
    The flames leap high and higher;

The rattling engines come too late:
    The old First Church is on fire!

And lo and behold, in the lurid glare
    They see John Carman stand,—
A look of mirth on his iron lips,
    And a blazing torch in his hand.

"You say it was *He* who killed her"
    (His voice had a fearful sound):
"I'd have you know, who worship Him so,
    I've burned His house to the ground."

            *   *   *   *   *   *

John Carman died in prison,
    In the madman's cell, they say;
And of his crime, that I've told in rhyme,
    Heaven cleanse his soul, I pray!

A Preacher

"And oh, my friends," the Preacher said, "beware,
    However smooth and tempting seems the path,
    With bowers of cooling shade, the end is wrath;
    Here 'tis unsafe, that's dangerous footing there:
But follow me and have no further care;
    I'll be your staff, for I am one that hath
    Lived long and gathered in life's aftermath—
    Experience. I bid you not despair;
Reach me your hands and cast away all doubt;
    I'll lead you safe along the glacier's shelf:
      You say 'tis dark? 'Tis noonday, I insist;
Besides, I know each pitfall hereabout,
    I know each chasm"—just then the Preacher's self
      Stumbled and plunged into eternal mist.

OCTOBER SUNDAY

Here are mellow October days;
Through my open window the organ plays
Out of the church across the road,
Leaves and people thickly strowed;
Those have done with every season,
These still live and seek the reason.

Organ-breath has drawn them in,
Souls that in an eddy spin,
Lifted upward from the clay:
In the road the leaves at play
Spin without the sap of passion,
Faded tints of Nature's fashion.

And what the organ says they drown,
Past my window whirling down
In sere pretence of keeping tryst;
So some bars of chords I've missed;
Now the wind has caught the strain
And drops the leaves, and listens fain:
For the souls a sweet wind borrow
To intone of earth's tomorrow.

When the road is still I hear,
Like crushed grapes, the notes of cheer;
When from these million tongues of leaves
The wind dead Pentecost receives,
I wait, the organ builds the while;
'Twixt me and the eternal smile
A scurry flits: but, tone-piers sinking,
Psalmward across I go unshrinking.

THE UNSEEN PREACHER

He spoke of souls that stooped and sinned,
    Of hearts that turned to roam;
He spoke of human restlessness,
    Of exile and of home,

Of earth's eternal vagrancies.
    "O slow!" he cried, "to start
And throw thy truant childhood back
    Upon thy Father's heart.

"That life must walk uncomforted,
    That leans not on His breast:
They only know that God is Love
    Who learn that God is Rest."

He spoke, and on his lifted face
    The prophet's halo crept:
Like reeds within his outstretched hands,
    The people bowed, and wept.

But in the chancel's solemn shade,
    She saw a glamour sweet.
"Beloved!" said she, "was it *you*
    Fled by with flashing feet;

"Across the holy desk and book,
    Beside the holy man,
Swift as a thought, and silent as
    Only the vanished can;

"Passed and stood listening, poisèd there,
    All in a dream of light,—
Paused to attend the sacred Word
    As only a spirit might?

      GEORGE PARSONS LATHROP

"As angels must, then, pity me,
　　So tempted and so blessed!
And teach me how, O loved and lost,
　　To go to *Him* for rest!

"Oh teach me how, when any world,
　　Or dark, or bright, or dim,
Containeth thee, to give my first,
　　My best of love to Him!"

CHILDREN'S SONG

Now the trees are on the air,
Now the flowers are in the vale,
Now the earth shows sweet and fair
    As our mother's tale.

Bright is every violet's eye,
Yellow-deep the cowslip hues,
Where the wide-winged butterfly
    Feeds herself with dews.

But the rising wind away
Turns the flower-bells bending low,
And the thunder-clouds do say
    Their sublimest now.

Leaps the flashing sword of light,
Rushes breeze and hisses rain;
Yet the trees are laughing bright
    At the watery gain.

        GEORGE PARSONS LATHROP

Amy Margaret

Amy Margaret's five years old;
Amy Margaret's hair is gold;
Dearer twenty thousand fold
    Than gold is Amy Margaret!

"Amy" is friend—is "Margaret"
The pearl for crown or carcanet!
Or peeping daisy, Summer's pet?
    Which are you, Amy Margaret?

A friend, a daisy, and a pearl,
A kindly, simple, precious girl,—
Such, howsoe'er the world may twirl,
    Be ever, Amy Margaret!

"My Heart, I cannot still it"

My heart, I cannot still it,
Is a nest with song-birds in it;
And when the last shall go,
The dreary days, to fill it,
Instead of lark or linnet
Will bring dead leaves and snow.

And were they sparrows only,
Without the passion stronger
Of joy that soars and sings,
Woe's me, I shall be lonely
When I can feel no longer
The impatience of their wings!

The Robin's Song

When the willows gleam along the brooks,
And the grass grows green in sunny nooks,
In the sunshine and the rain,
I hear the robins in the lane
    Singing, "Cheerily
        Cheer up—cheer up;
    Cheerily, cheerily
        Cheer up."

But the snow is still
Along the walls and on the hill.
The days are cold, the nights forlorn,
For one is here and one is gone.
    "Tut, tut. Cheerily
        Cheer up, cheer up;
    Cheerily, cheerily
        Cheer up!"

When spring hopes seem to wane,
I hear the joyful strain—
A song at night, a song at morn.
A lesson deep to me is borne,
    Hearing, "Cheerily
        Cheer up, cheer up;
    Cheerily, cheerily
        Cheer up."

THEOCRITUS

Ay! Unto thee belong
The pipe and song,
Theocritus,—
Loved by the satyr and the faun!
To thee the olive and the vine,
To thee the Mediterranean pine,
And the soft lapping sea!
Thine, Bacchus,
Thine, the blood-red revels,
Thine, the bearded goat!
Soft valleys unto thee,
And Aphrodite's shrine,
And maidens veiled in falling robes of lawn!
But unto us, to us,
The stalwart glories of the North;
Ours is the sounding main,
And ours the voices uttering forth
By midnight round these cliffs a mighty strain;
A tale of viewless islands in the deep
Washed by the waves' white fire;
Of mariners rocked asleep
In the great cradle, far from Grecian ire
Of Neptune and his train;
To us, to us,
The dark-leaved shadow and the shining birch,
The flight of gold through hollow woodlands driven,
Soft dying of the year with many a sigh,
These, all, to us are given!
And eyes that eager evermore shall search
The hidden seed, and searching find again
Unfading blossoms of a fadeless spring;
These, these, to us!
The sacred youth and maid,
Coy and half afraid;
The sorrowful earthly pall,
Winter and wintry rain,

And Autumn's gathered grain,
With whispering music in their fall;
These unto us!
And unto thee, Theocritus,
To thee,
The immortal childhood of the world,
The laughing waters of an inland sea,
And beckoning signal of a sail unfurled!

MEDALLION HEADS

(in six sonnets)

I

Saskia

The lovely Friesland maiden whom the pride
Inherent in her old patrician race,
Forbade not to renounce her birthright's place,
And seek her marriage bliss at Rembrandt's side,
Had recompense to Friesland's best denied:
For, never wearying of the auroral grace
Of Northern lights that flashed about her face,
He, for all time, her beauty glorified.

Her soul lies mute on each Madonna's mouth;
Her blonde hair floats across Bathsheba's breasts;
Her mingled snow-and-roses kindle up
Susannah's cheeks; as Hagar in her drouth,
She droops; and 'mid Ahasuerus' guests,
She sits, Queen Esther with the jewelled cup.

II

La Fornarina

Who can believe that he was thralled by *this?*
This creature wrought of flesh not over fine,
With brazen brow, and mouth whose sensual line
Holds no red sting of rapture in its kiss?—
This splendid animal, for whom life is
Mere pleased existence, pagan, undivine,—
Without a glimpse of soul, without a sign
That she could fathom the soundless depths of his?

We see the legend on her armlet traced,
"*Raphael Urbinas:*" yet deny that one
So born for love, so gracious, calm, and sweet,
So like a glad Greek god with beauty graced,
Could yield to toils by such Calypsos spun,—
Could stoop at such an earthly woman's feet!

III

Frau Agnes

From page to page they still repeat the wrong,—
How Agnes, with her shrewish marriage-ways,
Saddened the gentle Nuremberger's days,
Until the silken tie became a thong
Wherewith she pinioned him in bondage strong;
Yet who can lay his finger on a phrase
That proves it so? or cite a word's dispraise
Of her, his true "housereckoner,"[1] all life long?
One spiteful line has furnished forth the stuff
Whose hempen coil has strangled the fair name
Thus filched from Albrecht's wife, the centuries through;
For if the love she gave was not enough,
Or if his bosom nursed some fonder flame
That perished, surely Agnes never knew.

IV

Lucrezia

The pretty fool's face, with its white and red,
Its perfect oval, its bewitching pout,
The nimbus-shine of shimmering hair about
The Dian curve of brow, the well-poised head,
The rare-ripe, melting form, the princess' tread,
All lured his artist nature to devout

---

1. Dürer's playful designation, in his letters, of his wife.

Love for a siren, who that Art could scout
And barter for the gold it brought, instead.

Senza errori: Florence so did call
The Master Michael loved, and Raphael praised:
But when Lucrezia breathed her blighting breath
Across his faultless canvas, thenceforth all
His genius seemed to shrivel, till, hopeless, crazed,
His life's mistake found sole redress in death.

V

Vittoria Colonna

Serene and sad and still, she sat apart
In widowed saintliness, un unvowed nun,
Whose duty to the world without was done;
And yet concealing with unselfish art,
The scars of grief, the pangs of loss, the smart
Of pain, she suffered not herself to shun
The hurt, and bruised, and wronged, who one by one
Sought sanctuary of her cloistered heart.

But to that loneliest soul who found in her
His type of womanhood supremest set,
And knew not whether he should kneel or no,—
Such sweet, strange comfort did she minister,
That, were this deed her all, the world would yet
Have loved her for the love of Angelo!

VI

Quentin Matsys' Bride

An artist's daughter, she,—a toiler, he,
At the grim forge: all Antwerp well might stare
Upon him as a madman, that he dare
Aspire to hope, in face of the decree
Passed by parental pride,—that none should be

Received as suitor who should fail to bear
In hand—his own true work—a picture rare
Enough to prove his worth of such as she.

Yet nothing is impossible to Love:
 Soon through the city rang the cry abroad,—
"Behold the miracle of Matsys' saint!"
 Blind Genius felt Art's touch, as of a god,
 Had faith, and saw!—And tableted above
 Him still we read:—*"Love taught the smith to paint."*[1]
 Inscription on the Cathedral wall at Antwerp.

---

1. "Connubialis amor de Mulcibre fecit Apellem."

RED TAPE

What countless years, what wealth of brain were spent
To bring us hither from our caves and huts,
And trace through pathless wilds the patient ruts
Of Faith and Habit, by whose deep indent
Prudence may guide if genius be not lent,
Genius not always happy when it shuts
Its ears against the Plodder's ifs and buts,
Thinking by some brave leap to snatch the event!
The coursers of the sun, whose hoofs of flame
Burn through morn's misty threshold, are exact
As bankers' clerks, and all this star-poised frame,
Self-willed allowed, were with convulsion rackt:
The world would end, were Dulness not, to tame
Wit's feathered heels in the stern stocks of fact.

I Love to Dine

(Rondeau)

I love to dine when stains the sky one slender
Long line of wintry sunset; to the fender
    My back in close proximity; the *pâtè*
    Before me: I can watch the dying day,
And feel assured that the *rôti* is tender.

I can dine on a dollar—and the lender:
A haunch of venison, whosoe'er the sender:
    On general principles, yes, I may say
        I love to dine.

But most, when vis-à-vis the opposite gender
Is represented, with the repast to blend her
    Dear personality; when in one *purée*
    Our spirits mingle. Ah, that is the way—
When Love to Savarin stoops in sweet surrender,
        I love to dine.

THE BEAU OF THE TOWN

He once was young and gay—
    A beau.
(Ah, that was long ago!)
    Today
He is very old and gray.

His clothes were once the best;
    His tile
Was at the top of style;
    His vest
Was flowered upon his breast.

He then was tall and slim;
    His eye
Made all the maidens sigh
    For him—
One of the Cherubim!

He drove a handsome pair
    Of grays,
And all men sang his praise:
    The heir
Had plenty and to spare.

He now is poor and lame
    And bent.
His sunshine friends all went,
    And shame
To take their places came.

The flowers upon his vest
    Are rags;
His coat is green, and sags.
    The rest
May easily be guessed.

GEORGE PARSONS LATHROP

His youth was spent in vain;
    His age
Is like a blotted page:
    His bane
Was Roederer's Champagne.

Eumenides

He who in noblest strain Life's lessons uses,
Converts the avenging Furies into Muses;
Each dawn salutes with sweet surprises,
And cheerful thoughts ere he arises.
Him nothing sullens, nor displeases,
Nor vexed with life, nor dread diseases.

Fate is but Freedom with averted face,
Confront the demon and she flees apace:
Perplexed with life we only move
As dragged by strife or drawn by Love:
Souls that to love and truth are blind,
Ne'er enter forms of *human* kind.

ELD

All hail, thou Winter Solstice of man's life!
Lord of the faded flower and garnered sheaf,
That pluck'st from Time its nothings, leaf by leaf,
Cancell'st its troubles, dost annul its strife;
Thy scythe is sacred; healing is thy knife!
Small things thou tak'st: yet one thou giv'st—the chief—
In noble death our petulant raptures brief
Stilling, as organs still the lute and fife.
All hail, divine Detachment! When thy rod
Sweeps from the world its pomp, its praise, its pelf,
Say, what remains? The Pagan answered "Self":[1]
The Christian lifts his hands, and answers, "God."
All good our youth desired was God! Thou dim
Decline, find all things summed and sealed in him!

1. "Quid superest? Medea superest."
                    —SENECA: *Tragedy of Medea*

HORIZON

Oh subtle mystery of the air!
Or, is it mystery of the earth?
Which wooes? Which pregnant thrills to bear
In secrecy the beauteous birth?

Before the dawn from gray to rose,
Before the night from rose to gray,
With traceless change it comes and goes,
And comes and goes, and will not stay.

Our feet walk tireless in its lure;
Our eyes insatiate pierce its bound;
Our hearts wait confident and sure,
The wealth of its enchanted ground.

For threescore years from gray to rose,
From rose to gray, it shines and saves
Our lives from dearth.
            Who knows, who knows,
If we shall see it in our graves!

One Hundred and One

Concord, April 19th, 1876

How silent, sad, and gray
        The new-come April day,
And the tumult and the show of a year ago
        Already far away!

A single banner waves
        Above the ancient graves,
And the sleep is deep on the hillside steep,
        Where the chill wind runs and raves.

The plain, proud little town,
        Amid her meadows brown,
Sits lone again, and the great world's din
        Her thought no more doth drown.

That thought is not less high
        Than in the days gone by,
Though the mantle of honor be worn upon her
        Henceforth right soberly.

For still the quiet street,
        Where budding elms repeat
The whisper of the dead, high over head,
        Resounds to loyal feet.

Where youth died bravely once,
        Immortal youth in bronze,
Mid the strenuous urging of the spring-tide surging,
        Speaks with unfaltering tones.

And windows strait and high,
        Whence have looked on the sky
The eyes of sages, praying the ages
        For light and clear reply,

The common light receive,
Whereby all souls do live,
Whether the spirit charge inherit
To question or believe.

GEORGE PARSONS LATHROP

The Search

"Give me the girl whose lips disclose,
  Whene'er she speaks, rare pearls in rows,
  And yet whose words more genuine are
  Than pearls or any shining star.

"Give me those silvery tones that seem
  An angel's singing in a dream,—
  A presence beautiful to view,
  A seraph's, yet a woman's too.

"Give me that one whose temperate mind
  Is always toward the good inclined,
  Whose deeds spring from her soul unsought—
  Twin-born of grace and artless thought;

"Give me that spirit,—seek for her
  To be my constant minister!"
  Dear friend,—I heed your earnest prayers,—
  I'll call your lovely wife down-stairs.

Not Lost

Yes, cross in rest the little, snow-white hands.
　　Do you not see the lips so faintly red
　　With love's last kiss? Their sweetness has not fled,
Though now you say her sinless spirit stands,
Within the pale of God's bright summer lands.
　　Gather the soft hair round the dainty head,
　　As in past days. Who says that she is dead,
And never more will heed the old commands?
To your cold idols cling, I know she sleeps;
　　That her pure soul is not by vexed winds tost
　　Along the pathless altitudes of space.
This life but sows the seed, from which one reaps
　　The future's harvest. No, I have not lost
　　The glory and the gladness of her face.

Transfiguration

In Memoriam

Mysterious Death! who in a single hour
    Life's gold can so refine;
    And by thy art divine
Change mortal weakness to immortal power!

Bending beneath the weight of eighty years,
    Spent with the noble strife
    Of a victorious life,
We watched her fading heavenward, through our tears.

But, ere the sense of loss our hearts had wrung,
    A miracle was wrought,
    And swift as happy thought
She lived again, brave, beautiful, and young.

Age, Pain, and Sorrow dropped the veils they wore,
    And showed the tender eyes
    Of angels in disguise,
Whose discipline so patiently she bore.

The past years brought their harvests rich and fair,
    While Memory and Love
    Together fondly wove
A golden garland for the silver hair.

How could we mourn like those who are bereft,
    When every pang of grief
    Found balm for its relief
In counting up the treasure she had left?

Faith that withstood the shocks of toil and time,
    Hope that defied despair,
    Patience that conquered care,
And loyalty whose courage was sublime.

The great, deep heart that was a home for all;
   Just, eloquent and strong,
   In protest against wrong;
Wide charity that knew no sin, no fall.

The Spartan spirit that made life so grand,
   Mating poor daily needs
   With high, heroic deeds,
That wrested happiness from Fate's hard hand.

We thought to weep, but sing for joy instead,
   Full of the grateful peace
   That followed her release;
For nothing but the weary dust lies dead.

Oh noble woman! never more a queen
   Than in the laying down
   Of sceptre and of crown,
To win a greater kingdom yet unseen:

Teaching us how to seek the highest goal;
   To earn the true success;
   To live, to love, to bless,
And make death proud to take a royal soul.

IMMORTAL CLOUDS

O clouds, immortal clouds!
    You rise and float like flowers
Whose shaken dew might pour
    Through space, in perfumed showers.

Like flowers you bloom and fade;
    Like stricken hearts you tremble
And pass, yet seem to stay—
    So swift you reassemble.

O clouds, immortal clouds!
    With you I fain would wander;
So spirit-like you grow,
    Floating to Heaven yonder!

Pilgrims

"Have you not seen
In ancient times
Pilgrims pass by
Toward other climes?
With shining faces,
Youthful and strong,
Mounting this hill
With speech and with song?"

"Ah, my good sir,
I know not those ways:
Little my knowledge,
Tho' many my days.
When I have slumbered,
I have heard sounds
As of travellers passing
These my grounds.

'Twas a sweet music
Wafted them by,
I could not tell
If afar off or nigh.
Unless I dreamed it,
This was of yore:
I never told it
To mortal before,
Never remembered
But in my dreams
What to me waking
A miracle seems."

GEORGE PARSONS LATHROP

Avallon

I, Knight of Sorrow and Discontent,
Have been to the land of wonderment
   In a very far country.

The day was gone, the evening late:
A messenger came through the silent gate
   Of Dreams, and stood by me.

So fair a brow, so sweet a mien,
Had surely much of sorrow seen,
   And had found peace at last.

There was a kindness in his eyes,
And in the voice that said "Arise."
   Together, out we passed.

My comrade knights shall happy be
That these things happened unto me,
   The Knight of Discontent.

Strange was the land we travelled through,
Unpeopled, and no live thing grew
   Beside the tiresome way.

Upon the waste there fell no light
Of sun by day, or moon by night,
   But ever a twilight gray.

There was no sky, no wind did blow,
There fell no rain, there fell no snow,
Nor dew, nor frost the land did know,
   No change of cold and heat.

There is no winter—there no spring,
No summer-time, nor harvesting;

And dreary was our wandering,
And weary were my feet.

O, wait, my comrade knights, and see
Why these things happened unto me,
The Knight of Discontent.

Down to a river side we came,—
A river without source or name:
Its ceaseless current runs the same,
For ever and a day,

Around an island of great height,
Around an island of delight,
A peaceful island,—shining bright
With wondrous light alwày.

Mine eyes, that had been dim before,
Were blessed with visions on that shore,
Brighter than young men's visions, more
Than old men ever dream.

O throng of knights, thrice happy ye,
That these things happened unto me,
The Knight of Discontent.

I saw the mountain-isle divide,
I saw the high hills thrust aside,
And fair the valley open wide,
From centre to the stream.

At rest beneath the violet sky,
I saw its groves and cities lie,
More beauteous than human eye
Hath seen, or heart conceived.

There saw I mystic things, foretold
And written in the books of old,

Hintings of prophets overbold,
    By perfect faith believed.

A tree whose leaves will heal all harms,
The seven lamps with seven arms,
And new-named people bearing palms
    Were in that valley there.

And, while I gazed, desire awoke
To cross to those palm-bearing folk.
I seemed to turn not as I spoke:
    "Why stop we? Let us fare

"Unto that valley." But my guide,
That I had thought was close beside,
Stood far upon the flowing tide,
    And said: "Not yet for thee

"Comes there a sound of dipping oar,
"Comes there a boat from yonder shore:
"Not thee alone we wish, but more,"
    And, "Go thou back and see

"Of all the Knights of Discontent,
"The sorrow-bowed, the trouble-bent,
    "How many there may be

"To rise and put their armor on,
"And seek the vale of Avallon
    "In a very far country."

O listening knights, thrice blessed are ye,
That these things happened unto me,
    The Knight of Discontent.

Success

Success is counted sweetest
By those who ne'er succeed.
To comprehend a Nectar
Requires the sorest need.
Not one of all the Purple Host
Who took the flag today,
Can tell the definition,
So plain, of Victory,
As he defeated, dying,
On whose forbidden ear
The distant strains of triumph
Break, agonizing clear.

GUY VERNON

A NOVELETTE IN VERSE

Part I

THE WEDDING JOURNEY

I

He was as fair a bachelor as ever
    Resolved to take a wife at forty-five.
Indeed, how one so amiable and clever,
    Good-looking, rich, et cetera, could contrive
    Till the high noon of manhood not to wive,
Was a vexed theme, and long remained a mystery
To those who did not know his early history.

And none knew that among his bride's relations.
    At Saratoga, where you meet all grades
Of well-dressed people spending short vacations,
    Manœuvring mothers, marriageable maids,
    And fortune-hunters on their annual raids,
He saw her waltz, and spite of every barrier
Of years or influence, inly vowed, "I'll marry her!"

Barriers there were: she was but two-and-twenty,
    He, twice her age, as I have intimated.
But that seems no great matter: there are plenty
    Of wives today felicitously mated
    With husbands whose nativities are dated
(I speak with some authority) a score
Of years before their own, and sometimes more.

One barrier in himself quite good and strong
    There was,—the mystery no one could discover
Which kept our beau a bachelor so long:
    But when a man is very much a lover
    Such things are somehow easily got over:—
And one in her, on which he had not counted,
That could not be so readily surmounted.

The lady—though Guy Vernon did not know it—
  Had left another lover in the city,—
Rob Lorne, a journalist, and sort of poet;
  A fellow so unthrifty and so witty,
  That honest people said it was a pity
A needle of such point should have a head
Too fine to take a strong and useful thread.

While for a season they were separated,
  And in his dismal editorial den
The lover labored and the lady waited
  For him to make a fortune with his pen,—
  A thing which does not come to scribbling men
So often as, for one, I wish it did,—
Vernon stepped up and made a higher bid.

II

Guy Vernon's hand! a splendid offer truly!
  And though Florinda (so the muse shall name her)
Was neither false nor fickle, nor unduly her,
  Given to the world,—which never quite could claim
  Much as she loved society,—don't blame her,
If, when a man like Vernon wished to bid her in,
She thought the matter worth, at least, considering.

Good family, good habits, handsome presence,
  Breathing in dress, smile, gesture, look, and tone
That indefinable ethereal essence
  Of culture and high breeding,—let alone
  His private charities, which were well known,—
A match he seemed in everyway superior
To him whose chances chanced to be anterior.

Her friends all chorused, "Vernon!—Hear to us!
  A man of soul and sense is always young!"
But conscience whispered, "Plighted troth!" While thus
  Long time in even scale the battle hung
  (As somebody has somewhere said or sung),

Her heart—or shall we say imagination?—
Was in a fearful state of perturbation.

If she had been excessively in love,
    The business would at once have been decided.
The one imperious, mighty power, above
    All others in such matters—though unguided,
    Misguided often, scorned, profaned, derided—
Is Love, whose little arrow seldom fails,
Thrown in, to turn the matrimonial scales.

The trouble is, we do not love: who loves
    With that immortal passion, pure, supreme,
Strong and unselfish, tender as the dove's,
    Which touches life with a celestial beam,
    And wraps the world in its own radiant dream;—
Makes heavens of eyes, and then has power to bring
All heaven within the horizon of a ring?

III

One loved, at least,—our poet. How he first
    Learned of the complication, I've no notion;
But sudden lava-flood and flame outburst,
    A young volcano in Love's summer ocean,
    Which sank as suddenly; and, all devotion,
Humility, despair, self-sacrifice,
He wrote: "The world was right! you were not wise,

"To link your fate with one so poor as I:
    You're free." And after many tears, and blind,
Swift gusts of passion, she accepted Guy.—
    All which sounds commonplace enough, I find.
    But somehow it seems better, to my mind,
The muse should be a trifle too familiar,
Than pompous, adipose, and atrabiliar,

Singing the past in those false tones I loathe.
    Some poets seem oppressed with the conviction,

That to be classic, they must still re-clothe
    The venerable forms of antique fiction
    In what they deem approved poetic diction;
And so they let their unpruned fancies roll
Round some old theme, like hop-vines round a pole.

Give me the living theme, and living speech—
    The native stem and its spontaneous shoots,
Fibres and foliage of the soul that reach
    Deep down in human life their thrilling roots,
    And mould the sunshine into golden fruits,
Not ashes to the taste, but fit to feed
The highest and the humblest human need!

O singers of the sunset! is there naught
    Remaining for the muse, but just to fill
Old skins of fable with weak wine of thought?
    The child, Imagination, at his will
    Reshakes to wondrous forms of beauty still
A few bright shards of common joy and hope,
And turns the world in his kaleidoscope.

IV

Well, they were married, sometime in the autumn,
    At her aunt's house in town, with great display;
For though the bride was penniless, and brought him
    Her beauty for sole dower (that proud array
    Of lace and diamonds was his gift, they say),
A multitude of friends conspired to render
The wedding feast a perfect blaze of splendor.

She did not know, before, she had so many
    Rich and enthusiastic friends: the snob,
Who never would have sacrificed a penny
    In bridal gifts for one who married Rob,
    Made haste to join the fashionable mob,
Since Vernon was the man, and would have given his
Last dime to buy her something nice at Tiffany's.

Lorne bravely stood his ground till all was over;
    Then quietly looked round him for some means
Of burying his dead hope; became a rover,
    Visiting foreign countries and strange scenes;
    And, writing verses for the magazines,
Newspaper sketches, stories, correspondence, he
Struggled with his hotel-bills and despondency.

The wedded pair went off to Louisiana,
    Where Vernon owned a very large plantation,
And wintered in New Orleans and Havana,—
    A season of delightful dissipation,
    Sight-seeing, dining, driving, conversation,
And—best of all—the infinite variety
Found in each other's ever-fresh society.

A paragon of husbands; she admired
    His noble, courtly manhood more and more;
And everyday his constancy inspired
    In her a tenderer deference than before:
    So she began in earnest to adore
This married man and model of a hero,—
First love's quicksilver sinking fast to zero.

Such wedlock is, to true hearts truly wed;
    Love's guarded paradise; where sometimes they
Who enter with indifference or dread
    Find richest blessings; though I'm bound to say,
    The rule too often works the other way,
And disenchantment leads to evil courses,
Domestic jars, elopements, and divorces.

V

And all was lovely with our loving couple;
    Till, one day in Havana, there befell,
What seems a trifle, their first serious trouble.
    As they were riding on the Isabel
    Paseo, which the traveller knows so well,—

'Tis truly a magnificent parade,
Walks, fountains, statues, carriage-way, and shade;

Thronged with pedestrians, horsemen, prancing spans;
    Ladies in head-dress singularly scanty,
Darting dark glances from behind their fans,—
      Never on foot, but drawn (behind a jaunty
      Black-faced postilion) in a gay volante,
That Cuban gig, of easy jogging motion;—
Here, the fine harbor; there the circling ocean:

Epitome and picture of Havana,
    And that rich land of tropic fruit and tree,—
Fair Island of the orange and banana,
      And endless summer in a sapphire sea!
      Land of the cocoa and mahogany;
Voluptuous, balmy nights, and wondrous stars;
Of Creole beauties and the best cigars:

'Twas on that famous promenade, where daily
    You meet the wealth and fashion of the isle,—
As they were riding and conversing gayly,
      And now and then exchanging nod and smile,
      With new-made friends, along that marvellous mile,
In the soft, rosy twilight of the tropic,
Florinda touched upon a dangerous topic.

VI

Guy had a bright mulatto for a servant,
    A jewelled, gorgeous fellow; very handy
To pack a trunk, pay bills, discreet, observant;
      Originally nicknamed Sam or Sandy,
      But so superb and exquisite a dandy,
Resplendent in all sorts of gaudy things,
Florinda called him Saturn, for his rings.

Of all unfeathered bipeds,—Feejees, Negroes,—
    In any clime, of race refined or rude;

      GEORGE PARSONS LATHROP

Where crawls the crocodile, or where the tea grows;
  Pale, swarthy, tawny-skinned, or copper-hued;
  Turbaned or pigtailed, naked, furred, tattooed;—
The queerest yet turned out from Nature's shop
Is your complete, unmitigated fop.

And of all fops the foppiest yet was Saturn.
  'Twas rumored, he had once been Vernon's slave,
Now freed for his fidelity: a pattern
  Of your smooth, secret, serviceable knave;
  Guy's varlet, barber, purse, and very grave
Custodian of his cash, mustache, and collars;—
And worth himself some twenty thousand dollars.

Of her dear Vernon he was such a travesty;—
  The insufferable smile with which he asked
At what hour Guy would drive or dine or have his tea;
  The lazy insolence with which he basked
  In his own conscious gorgeousness,—so tasked
Florinda's patience and provoked her merriment,
That now she ventured on a rash experiment.

"I'm sick of such magnificence of vest!
  I hate the princely air with which he bends
That carded pate, oiled, scented! I detest
  Crinkled mustaches with waxed, pointed ends!
  But oh, I see!" she laughed, "the rogue intends
To have at least a few straight hairs about him.
Would the sky fall if we should do without him?

"Do please me, love,—get rid of this phenomenon!
  Dear, will you make me happy?" But although
The wish seemed not an idle, nor uncommon one,
  Vernon grew pallid, and with scarce a show
  Of his accustomed graciousness, said, "No!"
So bluntly, coldly, that her quick tears started,
And for five minutes she was broken-hearted.

"Darling!" she said, "I was but half in earnest;
    I only meant to say that—I can't bear him!"
"Unfortunate," he answered, with his sternest
        And most forbidding scowl, "for I can't spare him!"
        And, like the tyrant of a Turkish harem,
Thus having curtly uttered his conclusion,
He plucked his beard in anger and confusion.

But seeing her tears, he soon began to rally
    His gentler thoughts: "My dear, you do not know
That faithful, that incomparable valet,—
        A perfect nonpareil, as valets go!
        In other matters I am seldom slow
To heed your lightest wishes; but in such
A case as this you—really—ask too much.

"Reasons there are—but I can't undertake
    To give the reasons."—"Keep him, dear," she sighed;
"I'll even resolve to love him for your sake."
        And so the matter dropped: Florinda tried
        To make a jest of it, but only cried;
For Vernon's conduct, and the sallow fellow's
Strange influence with him, made her sad and jealous.

VII

So the ring'd planet kept his proud supremacy
    Over Guy Vernon's person, mind, and purse,—
As if there blazed not such another gem as he
        In the blue setting of the universe!
        And still Florinda liked him worse and worse;
But practised wise duplicity, concealing
With innocent art her inmost thought and feeling.

And all seemed well; till something far more serious
    Occurred her gentle tactics to derange:
First, something in the air, scarce felt, mysterious,
        The subtile shadow of a coming change;
        Then Guy grew restless, melancholy, strange,

GEORGE PARSONS LATHROP

Subject to absent moods and fitful sighs,
While Saturn watched him with keen, cautious eyes.

Florinda pleaded fondly: "Tell me, dearest,
    Your secret trouble! If you are in pain,
You know you have my tenderest, sincerest
    Sympathy,—which, I pray you, don't disdain!"
    But Vernon only groaned: "I can't explain!
Ask Sandy—there is something he will tell you."
And then abruptly left her with the fellow.

So the disgust and shame were forced upon her
    Of begging Saturn to unfold the matter.
He smiled, bowed, hand on waistcoat: "'Pon my honor!"—
    Quirking his eyebrows, he stood leering at her,
    Like some bedizened, over-civil satyr,—
"Extremely sorry—news from our attorney—
In short,—hem!—madam, we must make a journey."

"Where?" cries Florinda.—"Back to our plantation."
    "Tell me at once! what is the dreadful news?"
"The business scarce admits of explanation;
    For ladies, altogether too abstruse!"
    "When do we go?"—"Ah, madam! please excuse
The cruel circumstance, the—what you call
Necessity,—*you* do not go at all."

"And what becomes of *me?*" Pale, stunned, she stared.
    "Madam, you and your maid will be confided
To Captain Jones; so please you, be prepared
    To sail next week: all things have been provided."
    He smiled, extremely bland, but quite decided:
"Believe me, madam, 'tis with deepest sorrow
That *we* must sail—the other way—tomorrow."

She clasped her hands before him, speechless, trembling,
    Fearing some terrible distress or treason;
While Saturn stood there, simpering, dissembling.
    "Don't be alarmed,—you surely have no reason;

You join your friends, and later in the season,
    This trifling business ended, he will meet you.
Be calm, be patient, madam, I entreat you!"

She answered: "Tell me all—I will be calm!
    What is my husband's grief, this fearful trouble?
Money? a duel?" With a low salaam
    He bent his brilliant person nearly double
    (Body and soul seemed similarly supple):—
"Beg pardon, madam,—neither! To be brief,
Parting from you is his especial grief."

"Why does he leave me, then? O sir, be good!
    Is there another woman? Tell me truly!"
The fellow was a study as he stood,
    Grimacing, shrugging, lynx-eyed, white-toothed, woolly:
    "The circumstance has been explained as fully
As seems desirable,—but this I'll say,
No other woman stands in madam's way.

"Excuse me, madam, if I say no more.
    We go tomorrow, and you sail next week."
The rogue retreated, bowing, to the door,
    And adding,—"You'll do better not to speak
    To him of this affair, unless you seek
His ruin and your own unhappiness,"—
Left her in tears of terror and distress.

VIII

She flew to Vernon's room: abstracted, moody,
    Before his table, leaning on a chair,
Motionless, breathless, like a statue stood he,
    With drooping arms, bent head, disordered hair,
    In utter desolation and despair;
Then suddenly a shuddering sigh ran through him.
She stayed her steps, not daring to go to him.

Was this the noble Vernon she had wedded,
 The tender husband and the ardent wooer?
Unspeakably her poor heart longed, yet dreaded,
 To question, comfort him; when, turning to her,
 Quick as some conscience-stricken evil-doer
In his dark moments taken by surprise,
He glared upon her with strange, awful eyes.

Othello's thus on Desdemona burned.
 She took his hand, and silent, white with fear,
Yet, with the strength a strong heart gave, returned
 His lowering look, from large eyes deep and clear,
 Where love and pity trembled to a tear.
Then, as he smote his brow and turned away,
She asked, "Have you not one kind word to say?"

Strongly she held her wildly throbbing heart,
 Determined not to question nor complain;
But only said, "Tomorrow, then, we part?
 O Guy! dear Guy! when shall we meet again?"
 He wrung her hand until she shrank with pain;
Then flung her off, and from the chamber fled,
Leaving the little longed-for word unsaid.

IX

She felt her heart give way, and quickly grew ill,
 Sinking upon the couch in abject woe.
There as she lay, and thought how strange, how cruel
 That he should keep his secrets from her so,—
 That she had none which Vernon might not know,—
She started, thinking how she had forborne
To tell him of her love-affair with Lorne.

Now had some recent, terrible discovery
 Changed his regard to sudden deadly hate?
Oh! had she lost his love beyond recovery,
 Through that one fault, which unforgiving Fate
 Had left some loophole to reveal too late?

Was that malicious, treacherous, artful fellow
The dark Iago to her white Othello?

Was this his vengeance for that talk with Guy
    About his merits? Had some scrap of paper
Betrayed her secret? was her maid a spy?
    For thus in mystery's magnifying vapor
    The fearful soul sees giant shapes that ape her;
As in the Brocken spectre one discovers
One's own vast beckoning shade, that towers and hovers.

So Fear has oftenest but itself to fear.
    But though imagined ills are still the worst,
To troubled souls this truth is never clear;
    When evil lowers we deem the rule reversed,
    And fancy blacker woes about to burst
Upon our heads than any yet conceived.
So now Florinda, right or wrong, believed.

X

She rose and paced the room like one distracted;
    And wrote, but tore in haste the blotted sheet;
Then turned—I know not by what power attracted—
    To the front window-bars her restless feet,
    And, looking out upon the quaint old street,
Saw—with lithe head on graceful shoulders borne—
Her late, discarded lover, Robert Lorne:

Now habited like any Habenero,
    Sauntering as leisurely, quite free from care;
His fine face shaded by a light sombrero,
    Bearded, and brown as he had once been fair;
    Smoking his cigarito with an air
Of such observant fancy and enjoyment,
As seems your poet-traveller's fit employment.

He had not died of love,—that heart-disease
    Which proves but seldom fatal, to my thinking.

Defeated hope, sick fancy, if you please,
    Often induce a sentimental sinking,
    Drive some to suicide and some to drinking,
But stop far short of any such forlorn
And dismal end, with high, brave hearts like Lorne.

He had come down at first as far as Florida,
    And seen the alligator and flamingo;
Then, passing on to regions somewhat torrider,
    Reached the French-negro side of San Domingo,
    And learned a little of the curious lingo
The people speak there, but conceived no mighty
Love for those Black Republicans of Hayti.

He had at Port-au-Prince remained a while, and,
    With curiously well-furnished note-books, he
Was now returning by the greater Island,
    Which sweeps its curve of beauty thro' the sea;
    Where trade-winds temper the intensity
Of tropic heats—ah, would they might allay
The passions that distract the land today!

And so it chanced that he was now in town,
    And at this very moment passing by,
While poor Florinda stood there looking down.
    All which seems natural enough; but why
    He also chanced just then to turn his eye,
As if he felt the drawing of her glance,
Is a much more mysterious circumstance.

XI

At the long, open window, through the bars
    (Those Cuban fronts are formidably grated)
Burned her deep eyes, like two bright burning stars;
    Whereby it seemed that he was really fated
    To be for ever fooled and fascinated!
He started, turned half round, then, flushed and flurried,
Lifting his broad sombrero, on he hurried.

A dream, beyond all dreams of possibility,
    Her image there appeared! but none the less
The chance encounter jostled his tranquillity,
    And shattered, as you readily will guess,
    The new-filled crystal of his happiness;
As if a goblet, which he smiling bore,
Were dashed in fragments on a marble floor.

The tropic suns had not so scorched and wilted him
    As those two eyes! They left him trembling, weak,
Fevered and shaken, as when first she jilted him.
    He strode along with flaming heart and cheek,
    As if to find—what strangers need not seek
Long time in vain there, wandering up and down—
The mind's distraction in that novel town.

The place is picturesque with blacks and coolies,
    Peasants and panniered beasts: there's nothing odder
Than the slow-paced, half-hidden, peering mule is,
    Beneath his moving stack of fresh green fodder.
    It would be better if the streets were broader,
The windows glazed,—of that, though, I'm not sure,—
The hotels better, and mosquitoes fewer.

Lorne ranged the town; dined, spite of sentiment,
    Finished some correspondence for the morrow's
New Orleans mail; then hastened—with intent
    To make an article, and drown his sorrows—
    To see the town's renowned Plaza de Toros,
The place of bull-fights; for the first and last time
Assisting at the favorite Spanish pastime.

He must have been fastidious, not to fancy
    The frenzied multitude's vociferating,—
To wonder, as he did, what people *can* see,
    In frightening, torturing, and infuriating
    A poor dumb beast, so wildly fascinating;
What sport there is in all the shrieking, roaring,
Dart-piercing, spearing, bellowing, rushing, goring.

Departing with unspeakable disgust,
    In sea-baths sheltered from the prowling shark
He cooled his fever and washed off his dust;
    Walked the Paseo, spruce as any spark,
    Looking in all the carriages, till dark;
Then to the theatre—I blush to say,
Hoping to see Florinda at the play.

Nor novel scenes, nor all the blare and clamor
    Of bull-fights, nor the evening's promenade,
Nor sitting through a Spanish melodrama,
    Had power to make him anything but sad
    And irritated; for, alas! he had
No second vision of the eyes that haunted him,
Which being absent, nothing else enchanted him.

And so next day, in anger and despair
    Because he could not keep his truant thought,
And scarce his footsteps, from the window where
    That momentary glimpse of her was caught,
    Safety against his traitorous heart he sought,
And, to its mad attraction risen superior,
Made a short journey into the interior.

Part II

Homeward Voyage

I

Know ye the land?—and so forth. Cuba seems
    The later western Eden of our planet.
What wafted incense from the gate of dreams,
    What heavenly zephyrs hover o'er and fan it!
    With groves of orange, mango, and pomegranate,
And flowering forests through whose wealth of blooms,
Like living fires, dart birds of gorgeous plumes.

There by still bays the tall flamingo stands;
    The sunrise flame of whose reflected form
Crimsons the glassy wave and glistening sands.
    There, large and luminous, throughout the warm,
    Soft summer eves myriads of fireflies swarm;
Like the bright spirits of departed flowers
Nightly revisiting their native bowers.

Its own rich, varying world the isle enfolds;
    Where glowing Nature seems most prodigal
Of life and beauty; where the eye beholds
    Orchards that blossom while their ripe fruits fall;
    Mountains, refulgent vales; and, curved round all,
From some palm-crested summit seen afar,
The gleaming ocean's steel-bright scimitar.

II

All which to Lorne was an intoxication,
    That fed his passion while it soothed his pain.
Round aromatic jungle and plantation,
    Gardens of shaded coffee, seas of cane
    Sweeping their billowy verdure through the plain,

He breathed the flame of indolent desire,
And carried in his heart those eyes of fire.

She was unhappy! in the look she gave him
    Deep sorrow made impassioned, sad appeal.
So love conspired with pity to enslave him,
    And the sweet hope that still her heart might feel
    The heavenly hurt which only he could heal!
Until at last this new infatuation
Became an irresistible temptation.

Back to the city, with a wretched sense
    Of his own guilty weakness, in a tremor
Of passionate haste and torturing suspense,
    To meet her, flew the miserable dreamer;—
    But saw, just coming into port, a steamer,
At whose proud peak the Yankee ensign waved;
While something seemed to whisper, "You are saved!

"Fly! fly!" it said: "there is no middle course!
    Your coming cannot help, but only harm her.
Rally your manhood's enervated force,
    Put on determination's burnished armor!
    Sin is the lovely snake, the deadly charmer;
The tempted soul, the bird that round it hovers;
Flight, the sole safety for sore-tempted lovers!"

All which was seconded by sober reason,
    Making his duty in the matter clear:
'Twas late in February, and the season
    So dangerous to the northern blood was near;
    The best hotels were bad and very dear:
So Prudence, joined with Virtue, bade him leave her,
Avoid expense, temptation, and the fever.

Subtler considerations, too, assisted,
    No doubt, to make him do as he was bidden;
For conduct is a complex cord, that's twisted

Of many a strand of motive, seen or hidden,
   And sometimes with the weightiest purpose slid in,
And covered perfectly from tip to tip,—
The belly that gives vengeance to the whip.

With Lorne, this may have been deep-wounded pride
   And love's despite: "She shall not say I sought her!"
And so, his passport claimed, "Farewell," he cried,
   "Queen of the Isles, Spain's ill-adopted daughter!
   Farewell your plumy palms and blue sea-water!
Your toiling slaves and idle señoritas,
Paseos, chain-gangs, bull-fights, and mosquitoes!"

III

'Twas really when the steamer sailed next day,
   That Lorne, on board her, breathed his last farewell;
When from the port with countless streamers gay,
   By frowning bastion and tall citadel
   They passed, and took the grand Atlantic swell
And freshening sea-breeze, which are always found
Exhilarating to the homeward-bound.

He paced the deck, and puffed his cigarito,
   'Mid oranges in many a fragrant pile
(Barrels of oranges, stacked crates of ditto),
   And watched the gorgeous sunset's golden smile
   Fade on the lovely, fast-receding isle,
Then the soft, purple-pinioned twilight sweep
The dark-green land and iridescent deep.

Castles and villas, hills and plumy palms,
   Vanished, to live for ever in his view
Enring'd in rosy equinoctial calms.
   The burnished waves wore many a wondrous hue;
   Stars twinkled in the deep eternal blue;
And on the horizon of the sea, behold
The Southern Cross, with nails of burning gold!

GEORGE PARSONS LATHROP

IV

The waves, the heavens, the soothing, bland sea air,
    The beauty and the life, within him stirred
Depths of delicious longing, sweet despair;
    And gazing landward till his vision blurred,
    He breathed farewell to *her*. But now was heard,
Passing along the lower deck and upper,
A welcome call; and he went down to supper.

With excellent appetite, if one must know it,
    Which at the long, well-lighted cabin table,
Crowded with hungry passengers, our poet
    Was solacing as well as he was able,
    When, glancing round the clattering, chattering Babel,
He paused, aghast,—a slice of tongue half swallowed,—
Seeing the Fate which, flying, he had followed!

Florinda! pale but lovely still; enrapt in
    The delicate discussion of cold chicken,
And some engaging topic with the Captain.
    Just then, amid loud talk and teacups clicking,
    Over the wing she happened to be picking
She looked—and there was Lorne, quite dazed and pallid,
Staring at her across a dish of salad.

He was a sort of picturesque Adonis,
    With eyebrows of the true Adonis curve;
Eyes all expression; brown hair waved upon his
    Broad, graceful brow; fine nostrils, full of nerve;
    And something in the pure face that might serve
To make you like what still you might condemn in it,
And left him beautiful, but not effeminate.

Their eyes met for a moment; and the lady's
    Flashed on him, with a sudden dilatation,
Such grateful, radiant, sweet surprise as made his
    Whole being tremble with deep agitation,—
    Gave his quick spirits a singular elation,

And mantled his white forehead with a flush
Which deepened to a quite decided blush.

She did not blush (men often blush, somehow,
    When women don't): those eyes divinely bright,
Beneath the beaming crescent of her brow,—
    Venus's glow beside Diana's light
    (I trust my classic metaphors are right),—
Shone lustrously upon him, while his gaze
Sank modestly before their melting rays.

V

Ere long she rose; and, pausing just to turn on
    Poor Lorne a parting look, away she swept.
Where, all the while (he marvelled),—where was Vernon?
    Sea-sick, perhaps, and so his room he kept.
    Lorne's thoughts were flame: he sought the air, and stept
Up the steep stairs as light of heart and proud
As if he had been climbing on a cloud.

Now in the night he found a deeper charm;
    And to and fro he passed with pensive pace,—
When, lo, Florinda on the Captain's arm!
    He knew her by her shape of perfect grace,
    Then by the moonlit beauty of her face,
And soft, low accents, as they passed him by,
And found a seat beneath the open sky.

They passed—but what was that his ears had heard?
    Vernon not with her—gone to his plantation!
Never before had simple, spoken word
    Struck all his heartstrings into such vibration.
    But four months married, and a separation!
And she so pale! could there have been a quarrel?
He queried, with an interest quite immoral.

Now here were they, old lovers! For a minute
    He questioned his poor flattered conscience, whether

GEORGE PARSONS LATHROP

The hand of Providence might not be in it.
    That they should thus be voyaging together
    In the luxurious, lulling, lovely weather,
Just after he so virtuously had shunned her,
Appears indeed a matter of some wonder.

What was the Voice that hurried him aboard,
    He deemed his better angel's? Providence
Seems after all a sort of two-edged sword,—
    Now the direct, miraculous defence
    Of piety and helpless innocence;
Then, suddenly reversed, it seems no less
To shape the ways of sin and wickedness.

Could we but know when life's true light is given!
    Are there attendant powers of good and evil,
One Influence, rightly deemed the Will of Heaven,
    And one which we—in phrase not quite so civil—
    Succinctly term temptation of the Devil?
And both so like! Would someone, who has seen them,
Might teach us to discriminate between them!

Here, things are so astonishingly mixed,
    And morals still so little understood,
It takes a saint indeed to choose betwixt
    The bad that's pleasant and the bitter good,
    Always with perfect faith and certitude!
Evil, perhaps, being nothing more nor less
Than good in disproportion, or excess.

Impartial nature fosters and upholds them
    By the same equal laws, and it may be
The same great brooding power of Love enfolds them,
    With the vast patience of eternity!
    The beams of Life are laid in Harmony;
In whose triumphal, everlasting glory
Discord shall be resolved.—But to our story.

Lorne meant to show a dignified reserve
    By walking at a cool, respectful distance;
But towards Florinda still his feet would swerve,
    Drawn by a power beyond him, whose persistence
    Found in him little and still less resistance,
Till, starting with the Captain from their place,
The lady met him almost face to face.

Pure accident, of course. She bowed—quite slowly,
    As if her eyes might possibly deceive her.
With proudly meek, magnificently lowly
    Obeisance, under his uplifted beaver,
    He passed aside as if inclined to leave her.
Regardless of his coldness or his scorn,
She cried, "Why, truly! it is—Robert Lorne!"

Which he acknowledged, with another bend
    And civil show of passing. She detained him;
And introduced the Captain to her "friend";
    And still with silvery eloquence enchained him,
    And with a charming petulance arraigned him
For visiting the Cuban capital
Without so much as giving her a call!

"My husband would have been right glad to meet you!
    You came to Cuba—tell me when and how!"
"Excuse me," said the Captain,—"let me seat you,"—
    Placing a pair of camp-stools:—"I've just now
    Some duties which will take me to the bow."
And, seeing Robert and Florinda seated,
That guileless instrument of fate retreated.

They took their places mutely, without protest,
    And sat as if they had been carved in stone.
For hearts estranged, as you perhaps have noticed,
    When brought together and thus left alone,
    Cannot so easily resume the tone

Of light society, which often covers
The aching wounds of parted friends and lovers.

He who from his late Cuban trip had come
    Back to the town to seek her in such haste,
Now in her presence sat constrained and dumb;
    And he who fondly many a time had placed
    A lover's arm about that lovely waist,
Was strangely now become, while sitting by her,
A man of outward ice and inward fire.

The lady was the first to speak, of course.
    "You hate me, Robert!"—accents quick and low.
He answered in a voice repressed and hoarse:
    "What reason have I?"—"O, you shunned me so!
    But, Robert, there are things you do not know!
Can't we be friends? I need a friend! O Rob!"—
Here she was interrupted by a sob.

Then hardly could he master the impassioned,
    Wild words that forced his lips: "Have you forgot—
Florinda!" But he checked himself, and fashioned
    In the firm moulds of prudent speech his thought,
    And told how he from first to last had sought
Her happiness: "And so," he vowed, "you still
Shall have my whole life's service, if you will."

They talked; and words brought kind alleviation
    Of pain to both, and in new friendship bound them;
And the sweet sense of reconciliation
    Diffused an atmosphere of bliss around them;
    Till quite too soon the Captain came and found them;
And, happy in her late lost friend's recapture,
Florinda left him to his new-found rapture.

VII

A golden shallop on the rim of Ocean,
    The new moon poised, a slowly sinking crescent.

With throbbing heart and steady heaving motion,
  Strove the strong ship: the deep was phosphorescent,
  And on through fiery billows of liquescent,
Immingled meteors, rolling them asunder,
She kept her course through all that night of wonder.

O dear, inconstant Seraph of Repose!
  Wing to the homes of woe thy downy flight;
Visit the couch of wretchedness, and close
  The aching sense that wearies of the night!
  But when immortal Freshness and Delight
Sail with the enraptured soul the glorious deep,
What have we then to do with thee, O Sleep?

Remembering all her words, her looks, her sighs,
  Lorne vowed: "I will not wrong her; Heaven! I swear
For her sake endless love and sacrifice!
  Just to be near her, and to breathe the air
  She blesses with the fragrance of her hair,—
To shiver at the rustle of her dress,—
Is more than other mortals' happiness!"

He would not change his lot for any other.
  She need not *love* him: he would only ask
To be a *little* dearer than a brother!
  No richer blessing, no diviner task,
  Than to defend and comfort her, to bask
A little in her presence, and so feed
At those bright beams his heart's eternal need.

Love lights all men and women; and all things
  In youth and loveliness to love invoke us;
And beauty is a burning-glass that brings
  The soft, diffusive sunshine to a focus,—
  Whose rays, it may be said, sometimes provoke us
To kindle and consume with sweet desire,
While yet the glass feels nothing of the fire.

GEORGE PARSONS LATHROP

If she be cold, so much the worse for her!
    To be beloved is much; but far above
All that the whole world's worship can confer
    Of outward blessing, is the heart's own love,—
    Even that poor passion which adores a glove
Or lady's slipper,—though one's apt to find
Small solace in it, if she's *too* unkind.

VIII

Of all the wonders I have heard or read of,
    In these Centennial days and years of wonder,—
From this which tells us what the stars are made of,
    To that which over hemispheres and under
    The seas that hold the continents asunder
Speeds our swift thought,—of all, from first to latest,
The mighty Ocean steamship is the greatest.

To favoring gales it opens snow-white wings,
    But takes all gales with laughter; it salutes
Strange lands and climates in its course, and brings
    To northern shores full-ripened tropic fruits;
    A Titan, that to power and speed transmutes
Its daily ration of huge tons of coal,
And seems almost to be endowed with soul.

When I behold this little peopled world,
    Large as an asteroid, in the nether blue,
Its flashing wheels, proud decks, and flags unfurled;
    Then fancy that ancestral savage who
    First pushed from shore with paddle and canoe,—
I'm forced to the Darwinian conclusion
That here's a masterpiece of evolution.

From the first skiff of sutured skins or bark
    To the three-decker with its thundering guns,—
From Jason's classic junk, or Noah's ark,
    To the grand steamship of five thousand tons,—
    The thing developed: just as Man was once—

Well, not a monkey; that he never was—
But something less, evolved through Nature's laws.

Allah il Allah! great is Evolution,
    And Darwin eminently is its Prophet!
Out of primeval chaos and confusion
    It massed the nebulous orb, and fashioned of it
    The sun and planets; one whereof it saw fit
To finish off with most attractive features,
And make the abode of curious living creatures.

All which I do most potently believe,
    Taking large stock in Natural Selection.
But, gentlemen, I cannot quite conceive—
    Since centuries of plotting and reflection
    Have brought to pass the steamboat's last perfection—
What power, without intelligence or plan,
Evolved the wonders of the World and Man.

Not from without, 'tis true, with toil and din,
    Laboriously, the World was built or moulded:
By its own law, divinely, from within,
    No doubt, the incubated egg unfolded
    To the fledged miracle we now behold it.
Is thought evolved? then thought, I dare affirm,
Impregnated the primal cosmic germ.

Your gospel is a worthy contribution,
    Far as it goes; I thank you: yet I find,
Scanning the puppet-show of Evolution,
    A vast unoutlined Presence moves behind
    The wavering screen that hides the Will and Mind;
And shows, according as you take your stand,
More or less certain glimpses of a Hand.

IX

Trailing far back upon the blue Atlantic
    Its smoky banner; through the warm Gulf Stream

Rolling its white wake; with the slow, gigantic
    One arm of its for-ever-beckoning beam;
    Panting, with heart of fire and breath of steam,
The strong ship kept—as I set out to say—
Its steady northward course day after day.

The passengers, beneath the welcome shade
    Of awnings over all the vessel spread,
Fanned by the sea-breeze which their own speed made,
    Lounged half asleep, smoked, walked, and talked, and read,
    Or watched the flocking gulls that came and fled,—
Now circled close in quest of food, then fought,
Far back, about some morsel one had caught.

Two days of calm; when all the sea seemed one
    Vast fluctuating field of satin sheen,
Rolling and undulating in the sun,
    With evanescent gloss of gold and green:
    No land at last, not even a sail was seen,
Nor any steadfast thing to rest the eyes on,
Within the circle of the sea's horizon.

The bird of love, in days so truly halcyon,
    Upon the billows well might build her nest!
And then the nights! when flashed the moon's bright falchion
    Across old Ocean's palpitating breast;—
    When, watching, lingering later than the rest,
Our lover-friends, forgetting all prudential
Considerations, grew quite confidential.

He, rapt, devoted, with no thought of wronging
    Vernon or her: she, free from ill intent,
Needing the counsels of a friend, and longing
    For sympathy,—if that be innocent,—
    Confessed the dreadful, sudden, sad event,
Which, falling so mysteriously, bereft her
Almost of reason when her husband left her.

"We were so happy! I was just beginning
    To learn how dear he was!"—Lorne's spirits fell.
"O, do you think I've any chance of winning
    His love again?"—Poor Robert could not tell.
    "I've still *one* friend, thank Heaven!"—That pleased him well.
"I've never seen a happy moment since,
 And never shall again!"—which made him wince.

"What *do* you think—what *could* have been the trouble?"
    Revolving his conjectures, Lorne let fall,—
"The bursting of a speculative bubble."
    "I shall be happy yet, if that is all,
    And *he* is left me!"—Somehow this was gall.
"But oh, we never shall be reunited,
 I know!"—at which the villain was delighted.

"He may be—I'm afraid—" she hesitated:
    "That is, I hope, I trust it isn't true!"
"Some men get jealous," Robert intimated.
    "Jealous, I mean; and—how absurd!—of you.
    Oh dear, we must not sit here as we do,
And talk together!—Rob, it isn't right!"
But still they talked together, day and night.

And Robert wished (as many on like occasion
    Wish as devoutly) that the voyage might never
On earth arrive at any termination,
    But to the havens of bliss fare on for ever!
    Dreading the end, which all too soon would sever
This highly satisfactory arrangement,
And bring perhaps, with parting, fresh estrangement.

X

On the third morning something seemed the matter as
    Lorne went on deck: the winds were piping madly;
The ship was toiling somewhere off Cape Hatteras,
    Breasting the waves and spray, and pitching badly;
    Few faces seen, and those looked blue, and sadly

         GEORGE PARSONS LATHROP

Dispirited: with the rising of the seas,
The mercury'd sunk, some twenty-five degrees.

The call to breakfast—that sweet note of warning
    To hungry passengers—was something few heard,
And fewer still obeyed, that dismal morning.
    Here with his steaks came staggering up a steward;
    There—as they gave a sudden lurch to leeward—
A pale wretch, crawling in with some ability,
Shot out again with singular agility.

The dishes rattled and the coffee spilled,
    And over all, instead of general mirth,
A ghastly gloom the dreary cabin filled:
    No ladies seen,—the saddest thing on earth
    To Lorne; who, losing heart, back to his berth
Groped wretchedly, at length, and laid himself
Quietly on that dormitory shelf.

Of all things unromantic and accursed,
    To interrupt a pretty love affair,
Sea-sickness is the meanest and the worst!
    That is a woe devotion cannot share;
    Nor can one be expected much to care
Whether the hungry heart shall feed or famish,
When at each roll the stomach's growing qualmish.

For six-and-thirty hours the gale continued,
    And some weak souls on board had fears of sinking;
But still triumphantly the iron-sinewed,
    Grim Titan faced the billows without blinking.
    Lorne kept his berth, and passed the time in thinking,
In sending now and then to make inquiry
For someone's health, and scribbling in his diary.

Five days from port, at midday, they made entry
    Into Manhattan bay: the wind was bracing,
The storm had lulled, the skies were bleak and wintry,
    And strange appeared the leafless trees, the lacing

Of snows on roof and shore, so soon replacing,
To eyes filled with the south, the glorious calms,
The fruits and foliage of the land of palms.

The passengers, now muffled to the ears,
    Watched the slow steamer gliding to the dock,
The tugs, the lighters, and the ship-lined piers,
    The river ice in many a mottled block,
    And on a drifting mass the latest flock
Of gulls, just lighted, heading all one way,
Towards the cold wind that beat the ruffled bay.

Lorne lingered near Florinda, dull and dreamy:
    "And so we part!" he said. "But not for long,"
She answered sweetly. "You will come and see me—
    Tomorrow—soon—I know you will be strong,
    And not do anything that might seem wrong!
When one has friends, one wishes to be near them;
But folks *will* talk so,—'tis a shame to hear them!

"I shall be watched now, quoted, and reported.
    I'd have my independence if I could!
But, really, Rob, a woman can't afford it,—
    To have her motives all misunderstood!
    So now I'm sure you will be very good,
And not extend your courtesies too far,
But always seem—well, just the friend you are!"

Lorne was not happy: outwardly heroical,
    He helped her to a coach: she smiled: he bowed;
Then, with despair at heart, stood stern and stoical
    Amidst the beckoning, hauling, bawling crowd
    Of hackmen (so unreasonably loud!)
And watched the rattling vehicle that carried her
Back to her Brooklyn home, where Vernon married her.

GEORGE PARSONS LATHROP

Part III

The Forsaken Bride

I

Foreseeing all her friends' immense astonishment,
    Going to meet it with an equal dread,
Florinda gave her maid a strict admonishment
    Just what to say, and what to leave unsaid,
    To questions soon to shower upon her head;
For, first suspicions having proved unjust,
The girl was granted all the greater trust.

Deep was the dear old Aunt's amazement, meeting
    At the hall door the unexpected bride.
Then, having passed the first tumultuous greeting,
    "Your husband, Florie! where is he?" she cried,
    Still more bewildered; while the niece replied,
"Some sudden and important information
Obliged him to return by his plantation."

"Without his bride!" "Why, Aunt, 'twas getting late—
    'Twas not thought best that I should risk my health.
The owner of so splendid an estate
    Of course is burdened with the cares of wealth.
    In politics he mixes too—by stealth;
For he is quite above those sordid natures
That fill our congresses and legislatures.

"We came directly by the boat—so pleasant!
    I missed my dearest husband, I confess,
But—O dear Aunt! who do you think was present
    Among the passengers? You cannot guess!
    Surely there's no one *I* expected less
To see on board than Mr. Robert Lorne!
He treated me at first with downright scorn,

"As if I'd really done him some great evil.
    I could not speak to *him*, and why should *he* seek
An interview? But he at length grew civil,
    And sent his brandy-flask when I was sea-sick,
    (The lightest gale is certain to make *me* sick!)
An offer which I couldn't well refuse,
Though brandy's something which I never use.

"We had two days of most distressing weather!
    I could have envied martyrs on the rack.
I do not think I cared a pin's weight whether
    I lived or died!—I'm so glad to get back!
    Robert was kind, and helped us to a hack;
Of course I had to ask the man to call,
Or show him no civility at all."

Truth, every word; though it perhaps may strike
    The reader as too gingerly expressed.
Women and Truth, I find, depend alike,
    For their effect, upon the way they're dressed.
    I like for both a simple garment best;
But nothing can exceed a woman's tact
In fancy-dressing both herself and Fact.

Do not too hastily infer that woman
    Is guilty of downright equivocation.
It is not only feminine, but human,
    To modify by phrase and intonation
    Truth's simple theme, till, through the variation
Sometimes embroidered on the homely air,
You hardly guess what good old tune is there.

II

The bride, whose coming was a nine-days' wonder,
    Received in Brooklyn, where her court was held,
So many callers that they fairly stunned her;—
    Not old friends only; but her train was swelled
    By more whom love of novelty impelled,

And some who thought it worth their while to seek
The charming Mrs. Vernon for their clique.

With all the rest, but from a different motive,
    Went Lorne,—and but a sad appearance made he.
So have I seen a worshipper with votive
    Offerings approach some altar of Our Lady,
    To find a crowd of tourists there already,
Airing their guide-books, venturing praise or stricture
Upon this sacred relic or that picture.

The world soon wearies of a stale sensation;
    And as the swift weeks came and went without
Bringing Guy Vernon back from his plantation,
    People began to shake their heads, and doubt;
    Till something of the secret had leaked out,
One scarce knows how: a little, I'm afraid,
Came through the indiscretion of the maid.

With Robert Lorne's, Florinda's name was coupled
    In terms uncomplimentary to both.
And so discreet Society grew troubled:
    'Twas shocked, distressed: it pitied her; 'twas loath
    To think what had been told it under oath!
In short, it never, never could esteem her,
After her shameful conduct on the steamer!

"He followed her upon her wedding journey,
    And there in Cuba showed her such devotion!
Vernon was out one day: on his return, he—
    Well, all I know is, there was an explosion!
    Just what the man discovered, I've no notion;
I only say, he left her in Havana,
And hurried off next day to Louisiana,

"Cursing, no doubt, the hour when he was wedded!"
    Which was not white and stainless truth, we know,
But held some darker substances imbedded:
    Just one of Rumor's rolling balls of snow,

That pick up sticks and rubbish as they go:
The farther they are rolled, the more they gather;
And suburbs are the place for rubbish, rather.

This to Florinda was a fearful trial,
    Added to that which secretly she bore;
For now no explanation, no denial,
    Not truth itself, which might have served before,
    Could kill reports, but only raise up more.
In fine, her double-burden so unfitted her
For life itself that you would quite have pitied her.

A common scandal is a borrowed tool
    Passing from hand to hand, yet never losing
Its edge by any ordinary rule,
    Battered and blunted by severe abusing;
    But, like a cat's claw, it grows sharp with using;
Whose softer part wears faster from the friction,
Leaving the other keen, for your affliction.

III

No word from Vernon; though she wrote and pleaded
    Until that rascal, Saturn, must have laughed!
Her love and grief remained alike unheeded:
    But as each month came round, a princely draft
    Shot at her heart its cruel golden shaft;
And in the very thickest of the slander
There came a note from "Samuel Alexander."

For so the Varlet signed himself; and truly,
    A singular performance was this letter!
He begged to say that Mr. V. was duly
    Regretful that he must remain her debtor
    For correspondence until he was better:
He had been slightly ill of late; beside,
He was just then extremely occupied.

"The business which has brought us here" (I quote
    From Saturn's postscript) "is not yet quite ended."
Again, in Postscript Number Two, he wrote:
    "Be easy, Madam; he is well attended,
    And, everything considered, doing splendid!
Please, Madam, do not write again, but wait."
The missive, I should mention, bore no date.

'Twas a distressing riddle: heart and brain
    Were racked and puzzled by it many a day.
"He must be ill!"—but that did not explain
    His parting from her in that cruel way,
    His long, mysterious silence, and delay
On that strange business,—too much occupied
To write one line to his forsaken bride!

From her good Aunt she got but little solace,—
    A woman of confirmed opinions, blest
With little patience for a young girl's follies;
    Who doubted not her niece had lost the best,
    Most generous, most devoted, handsomest
Of husbands, through her own infatuation;—
But deemed the monthly draft a consolation.

Friends do not like to own that ever any
    Advice of theirs in any way was bad.
So in Florinda's circle there were many
    Who, though the sequel to the match was sad,
    Blamed her for all the ill success it had;
While others would not willingly admit
That ever they approved or counselled it.

The World, it may be said, dropped her acquaintance;
    But there were those who could not keep away,—
Who came to witness suffering and repentance,
    To talk the matter over everyday,
    To know just how she felt, what she would say:
So she had more than one friend who stuck by her,
Though something in the fashion of a brier.

IV

For Lorne the starry skies of Love had brightened
    When her full-mooned renown began to wane;
But soon the cloud of ill report had frightened
    Both back to their discreet reserve again.
    Hardly could he that stormy heart restrain,
Which sometimes drove him now—as if a very
Demon possessed him—down to Brooklyn ferry!

It was his own imprudence that involved her
    In this vile coil,—he thought with penitence.
How tenderly his own great love absolved her
    Of every fault but that sweet confidence
    Which proved to him her very innocence!
He burned to be her champion,—but forbore,
Knowing that he could only harm her more.

He plunged in work: his Southern notes he winnowed;
    And, much as he a mean deception spurned,
In corresponding with the press, continued
    To date from countries whence he had returned,
    If he indeed had seen them; and so learned
The art—imaginative and dramatic—
Of writing foreign letters from an attic.

His friends averred that he could never gain
    A handsome independence by his pen,
And marvelled why such genius should remain
    A beggar in a barren garret, when
    He might, like many far less able men,
Become a lawyer, or a politician,
And strike for office, fortune, and position.

V

His lodging overlooked, in the Metropolis,
    A narrow business street, not over nice,
But unromantically over-populous;

Where, much against the aforesaid friends' advice,
   He kept on writing at a moderate price,
Pieces pathetic, picturesque, or funny,
Which gained for him much credit, and some money.

One April afternoon, as he sat writing,
   Buried in books and papers to the chin,
Where the high luthern window let the light in,
   A hand—scarce heard above the incessant din
   Of the loud street—tapped at his door. "Come in!"
He shouted out, in tones not over-civil,
Expecting no one but the printer's devil.

Then, too intently occupied to stop, he—
   Still studying an unfinished period—
Over his shoulder reached a roll of copy,
   Giving a little sidelong careless nod;
   But thought the fellow's movements rather odd,—
Turned slowly,—gazed,—and just escaped capsizing
His loaded table in his hasty rising.

He stands and stammers, so confused and vexed is he
   At his own awkward blunder;—but, O heaven!
What sudden joy, what thrilling, boundless ecstasy,
   When from a woman's veil one glance is given,
   And, like a panting fawn to covert driven,
Pale, with a look of exquisite concern on
Her fair, sweet face, behold—Florinda Vernon!

VI

He sprang to meet her, eager hands outreaching
   To clasp, to bless her; but as he came near,
She started from him with a strange, beseeching,
   Wild look, in which there was a mingled fear.
   "O Rob," she cried, "I'm crazy to be here!
What would they *now* say if they only knew it!
I can't—myself—conceive what made me do it!

"I know you'll think me dreadfully immodest!—
    O Rob! it isn't a mere girlish freak!"
But here she paused, being so tightly bodiced,
    And out of breath from climbing stairs, and weak
    From agitation, that she could not speak;
When seeing her grow faint and gasp for air,
He thought at last to offer her a chair.

Her maid, in his place, would have guessed the matter,
    Have found her corset, and at once unlaced it.
But Rob could only stand there staring at her,
    And bring some sherry, begging her to taste it;
    Which she but touched, then on the table placed it;
And, having now recovered from her faintness,
Looked up at him and smiled with charming quaintness.

"This is a scene! I'm horribly ashamed!—
    You must not blame me!"—quickly growing serious.
"I'm stifled!—O dear!—Robert," she exclaimed,
    "I've come on business—something quite imperious";
    And, lest the lady's interlude should weary us,
We'll simply add that, while he sprang to get her
Some sort of fan, she pulled out Saturn's letter.

She talked to him about it while he read it,
    Fanning herself incessantly, and weeping;
Told him of all she suffered, all she dreaded:
    The mystery haunted her awake or sleeping;
    And, O, it never could be solved! Then, leaping
To a most sudden, woman-like conclusion,
She begged, entreated him for a solution.

VII

"Well, looking at it in a business way,"
    Said Lorne,—"as if I now first heard the tale,
And did not know the parties,—I should say
    Guy Vernon was a felon, out on bail;
    I think he's now convicted, and in jail.

Summoned to trial under his indictment—
That's what his strange despair and sudden flight meant,

"When he had hoped to quash it, all the time."
     "O Rob, you do not think so!"—"Well, why not?
It may have been some gentlemanly crime—
     A duel, and his adversary shot—
     The southern blood, you know, is quick and hot."
"No, no!" she cried, "that's not like him! The duellist
Is of all men, I've heard him say, the cruelest!

"He hates the code!—although at first I feared
     That he was challenged, and was going to fight.
But, grant it all, the mystery is not cleared:
     Why treat me so? and why could he not write
     One letter, even in jail?" Says Rob, "You're right."
And, on examination, thus they found,
That theory was not altogether sound.

"There is," said Lorne, "one other explanation—
     But that, I know, you will not like to hear.
And yet," he said, with painful hesitation,
     "No other seems to make the matter clear.
     Suppose he had been summoned to appear
And meet a different trial in his life?—
I mean, your husband has another wife."

This she opposed with vehement persistency.
     "O Rob, it is a monstrous thought!—O no!
And yet," she said, with feminine consistency,
     "He *must* have had another wife, I know,
     For nothing else could separate us so!
I did not think my husband was so bad!
Say something, Robert, or I shall go mad!"

"My dear!" cries Lorne, "'twas only a suggestion!"
     And yet the theory seemed not wholly wrong:
It answered, too, the old provoking question,
     What kept our beau a bachelor so long?

"The wretch," she sobbed, "was married all along!
He may have had a dozen wives beside,
And may be finding now another bride!

"And I am not his wife at all!"—Lorne trembled
　　At all these wildly uttered words implied:
Her hand was free, then! But his soul dissembled
　　Its secret joy; while he sincerely tried
　　To think but of her grief. "Why now," he cried,
"You're driving my conjecture quite too far:
'Tis only in romance that such things are.

"Vernon is not a murderer, nor a forger,
　　Nor jealous fool, as far as we can know;
Nor Bluebeard, looking for more wives to torture;
　　Nor bankrupt—as the drafts they send you show;
　　Nor varlet's tool and victim: far below
Our present knowledge and my comprehension
The mystery lurks, and baffles my invention!"

"You do not think," she said, "he is a gambler,—
　　That Saturn aids him in that horrid vice?
Or is he just a wanton, reckless rambler?
　　Never did I discover card or dice!
　　O Rob," she pleaded, "give me some advice!
Pity my wretched, my forlorn condition!"
And so, at last, he made this proposition:

"I have a correspondent,—George Lazell,—
　　A classmate and old crony,—studying law
There in New Orleans: I have known him well:
　　One of the quickest wits you ever saw
　　To prove a question or to pick a flaw.
I've not the slightest doubt he can unravel
This riddle, with a little time and travel.

"With your consent, I'll put him in possession"—
　　Florinda shuddered—"of the whole affair,
And leave its management to his discretion,

Which can be trusted: give him but a hair,
    And he will track the mystery to its lair,—
Work up the case, and leave no point neglected,
To keep your action in it unsuspected."

She first approved the plan, then straight repented:
    It would not do—she dared not! 'twas not right!—
Then, after many doubts and sighs, consented,
    And hurried home,—Rob promising to write
    The letter to his friend that very night;—
But she next morning sent a note to say
It must not go—when it was on its way.

VIII

Ah, then, for her what days of expectation,
    Of curiosity akin to fear;
Of baffled hope, and causeless trepidation
    At sound or sight!—a voice she chanced to hear,
    Perhaps the liveried footman drawing near,
Who came like Fate, and idly went his way,
Leaving a desolate and empty day.

The weeks went by and brought no revelation,
    And letters came she did not care to read.
But now she had one secret consolation,—
    And, O, what harm, if in her heart's great need
    She sometimes went to *him?* What harm indeed,
But that imprudence is the door to sin,
And one small fault may let large vices in.

To tempted souls there is delight in danger,
    And then the provocation seems complete,
When Marriage, like a mastiff in the manger,
    But guards the morsel which it may not eat,
    And Love and Daring find that morsel sweet!
Don't blame your wife too much, sir; but consider,
Perhaps your coldness or neglect undid her.

A little pressure of the hand, returning
    Another's pressure; eyebeams free as air;
The lonely heart's unutterable yearning,—
    All this even Innocence itself may share:
    And then a kiss is but a kiss—beware!
It is a little mouse that gnaws the net
Around a mighty lion: guard him yet!

The world is full of pining hearts mismated,
    And still they will mismate, and still will pine.
Is thy sweet hunger never to be sated,
    O Love? But Duty also is divine;
    And Passion finds a poison in the wine,
In secret, at a stolen banquet poured,
When holy Conscience blesses not the board.

On every side conflicting voices call;
    And we must reconcile as best we can
The rights of each and the great good of all,
    The claims of Nature and the laws of man,—
    The problem since Society began!
O troubled soul! be tender, wise, and true,
And 'tis beginning to be solved—for you.

Part IV

THE LOST BRIDEGROOM

I

Meanwhile Lazell accepted the commission;
    Though it was long before he could report.
He moved with all the caution and precision
    Of any practised diplomat at court,
    Or strategist advancing on a fort;
And 'twas no fault of his if something less
Was compassed than unqualified success.

All Lorne could tell him of the strange event,
    Or he himself could learn at Guy's plantation,
Or at the bank from which the drafts were sent,
    Or elsewhere, bearing on the situation,
    Was added carefully to his equation,
When, by no common difficulties daunted, he
Essayed to cipher out the unknown quantity.

II

He wrote to Lorne of everything, confessing—
    "It makes me, Rob, exceedingly dejected,
To find that here's a riddle there's no guessing
    From all the facts so carefully collected.
    The man is known, and everywhere respected;
If a great villain, he must be a rare actor,
Still to preserve so excellent a character.

"Here in the city, and at his estate,
    His friends, when questioned, commonly replied,
'We haven't seen nor heard from him, of late;
    But he was here last winter with his bride.'
    If he's here now, why, then, we must decide,

Be what he may, whatever else he lacks,
He has the art of covering up his tracks.

"I don't believe he's in these parts at all!
    I'm wrong, no doubt you think: perhaps I am:
For his man Alexander,—whom they call
    'Big Sandy' here, or sometimes 'Dandy Sam,'—
    That gorgeous graft upon the stock of Ham,—
Has been at V.'s plantation, and in town;
Though I could not contrive to hunt him down.

"I followed that embodied Will-o'-wisp
    From place to place,—in hopes to overhaul
A waistcoat and the waxed ends of a crisp,
    Pointed mustache: the trail was now so small,
    I vowed that he, too, was not here at all;
Then I could swear—so great the rumor grew of him,
And he was here and there so—there were two of him!

"'Twas now a flying visit to the bank
    On Vernon's business,—if indeed it be
Not more his own than Vernon's: to be frank,
    I've not the slightest doubt but it is he
    Who sends the monthly draft to Mrs. V.
In Vernon's name there is a large deposit,
But 'tis this Dandy Sam who always draws it.

"When I rushed in to catch him there, I learned
    That he was up the river, on the estate;
And though I had but recently returned
    From reconnoitring thereabouts, with great
    Celerity and caution back there straight
I sped, to pounce upon him like a cougar—
Pretending always to be buying sugar.

"It seemed as if some magic must have aided
    To screen a fellow of so great renown,
For he had vanished, somehow separated,
    And gone, part up the river, and part down,

Half to the northward, and half back to town:
So said two sets of persons who had seen him,
And it was just my luck to pounce between him.

"V.'s is the best plantation in the parish,
    Perhaps the very finest in the State;
The mansion, truly elegant, not garish;
    Yet Vernon never stays there long of late;
    And Sam—an object of especial hate
To everyone, from Cuff to overseer—
Comes only now and then to domineer.

"The people say that Vernon's with his wife
    Somewhere up North,—the general opinion.
I've learned from them a little of his life:
    He is by birth and breeding a Virginian,
    Who emigrated from the Old Dominion
Twelve years ago—if that be emigration,
To take possession of an old plantation.

"Of the Virginia servants two alone,
    Sam and an aged negress, now remain;
The latter very deaf: her wits have flown
    Back to the deepening twilight of her brain,
    So that, I find, there is not much to gain
By sounding that dim cave, to bring the bats
Zizzagging aimlessly around our hats.

"Yet somethings this old creature has let fall
    To others, which, whatever they may mean,
Are worth perhaps the trouble to recall:
    How Vernon's mother perished of some keen
    Heart-piercing anguish; and how she has seen
The father, ghastly pale, perspiring clammily
Over some fearful secret in the family.

"Whether that secret be the same as this
    Which we would fathom, can but be suspected:
For secret most assuredly there is,

And with it Sam is certainly connected;
    Whose will has so mysteriously subjected
His master's, that you hear it said, he runs
Vernon and his plantation both at once.

"This is by no means Mr. Vernon's first
    Mysterious disappearance, as I find;
Though, on his wife's account, it seems the worst
    And strangest case of absence of the kind.
    Suddenly he—or Sam—makes up his mind,
And, presto! like the slipperiest of debtors,
He's off, beyond the reach of friends or letters.

"So said, at least, my friend the overseer;
    Declaring in half-earnest, grisly fun,
'Twas his conviction, that for many a year
    Vernon at stated intervals has done
    Some private business with the Evil One,
Which claims, in spite of friendship or the ladies,
His personal attention down in Hades!"

Thus wrote to Robert Lorne the young attorney,
    To whom the curious case had been confided;
Adding, "Without another, longer journey,
    I fear the question cannot be decided.
    You may no doubt accomplish more than I did,
And gain some knowledge, or obtain some trace,
Of Vernon, on the Old Virginia place."

III

This letter, which had been so long awaited,
    Caused in the wife an easy transformation:
The fever-pulse of hope and fear abated;
    And with the lapse of high-wrought expectation,
    There came a sudden, dangerous relaxation
Of those firm principles which hitherto
Had kept her, through all perils, pure and true.

Now all her sinking, unsupported heart
    Reached out for love,—trembling and insecure.
And so one day she dressed herself to start
    Upon a fashionable shopping-tour,
    Which—one might safely prophesy—was sure
To have a rather un-aristocratic,
Impulsive ending, in a young man's attic.

A coach was called; and soon a coach came dinning
    Its music in her ears; and, pondering more
The journey's joyous end than its beginning,
    She hurried forth; but stopped, aghast, before
    Some legs in the just-opened carriage-door,
Which to her startled gaze so much resembled
A missing pair, that she stood still and trembled.

"Florinda!" said a voice; and someone, rising,
    Peered out—then even the sky turned black above her!
As well it might: what could be more surprising
    To the young wife, just going to meet her lover,
    Than thus inopportunely to discover
A terrible reminder of her marriage,
In her own husband stepping from a carriage!

IV

Fainting is commonplace, even in romances;
    So let us say that, after some disorder,
When she was lying on a lounge, and Nancy's
    Care—and cologne—had partially restored her,
    She heard a voice which tenderly implored her
To calm herself; and, opening her eyes,
Found that it was indeed her dear, lost Guy's!

She sat right up and stared him in the face,
    Half-doubtful if she really were beholding
Her husband or a spectre in his place,
    And half inclined to give him a good scolding;
    Then pulled away the hand which he was holding,

And dropped some passionate tears; but, for a miracle,
Was neither sentimental nor hysterical.

"Our sudden meeting has quite overcome you!
    You blame me! but you do not know how strong
Was the necessity which kept me from you.
    Although my absence has been strange and long,
    I've done no needless or intended wrong,
Believe me, love!"—a bit of an oration,
Too evidently studied for the occasion.

Even honest men, with something to conceal,
    Not daring quite to trust the impetuous heart
To speak directly what they deeply feel,
    Are sometimes tempted to prepare the part
    Which they are called to act, and at the start
Put on the spirit—so to speak—a manacle,
Which makes their words seem formal and mechanical.

'Twas thus with Vernon, if I err not greatly:
    His tongue was frigid, while his heart was torrid.
And when she saw him, elegant and stately,
    With calm locks brushed across his bald white forehead,—
    Still slightly corpulent and somewhat florid,—
In health, addressing her with all the awful ease
Of some well-combed and courtly Mephistopheles,—

As if the past were no such dreadful load,—
    She looked at him amazed, and almost frightened,
(Forgetting quite the little episode
    By which for her the burden had been lightened,)
    And felt the horror of the mystery heightened,
But neither made complaint nor exclamation—
Only her eyes demanding explanation.

V

"You were not looking for me in the coach?
    You did not get my letter, then!" She darted

At him a look of terrible reproach:
    "Never," she cried, and now the deep sobs started,
    "Never a line from you since last we parted!
Little I dreamed—when, yielding my consent,
I signed that dreadful paper[1]—what it meant!"

Just then the maid, a letter in her hand
    (She had been listening at the door until
That instant), entered: "This was on the stand;
    It must have come just now when you were ill."
    Florinda took it, but without a thrill:
The flowers of hope, which we too long await,
May lose their bloom and come at last too late!

Post-marked New Orleans, July twenty-third;
    The date conspicuously a fortnight older;
Written in Guy's fair hand (but not a word
    To show where it was penned), the letter told her
    How fondly he looked forward to behold her,
And prove his heart's devotion soon once more,—
Their trials passed, and happier days in store.

This missive, which she read through flashing tears,
    After its meagre contents were made out
She tossed to Guy; who colored to the ears,
    Comparing date and postmark: he no doubt
    (She thought) had mailed it in some roundabout,
Strange way, that his retreat might not be traced,
And afterwards outrun it in his haste.

Then suddenly the sense of her great wrong
    Possessed her; and—to make the story brief—
She sobbed so strongly, and she sobbed so long,
    It seemed her soul could never find relief
    To its wild, inextinguishable grief,

---

1. By the Cuban passport system—quite too strict in some points, but perhaps not in this—the husband who has lately taken his wife into the island cannot obtain his permit to leave without her, unless he first exhibits at the Bureau her written consent. Probably this is what Florinda alludes to.

Which sighs but fanned, and tears in vain might drench,—
Like that Greek fire which water will not quench.

VI

"Florinda!" said Guy Vernon, very grave,
    When she could hear him,—studying now no more
What he should say, or how he should behave,—
    "There's something which I should have said before—
    And would to Heaven that it might now restore
Our former happiness and dear repose,
Lost through no weakness of my heart, Heaven knows!

"When first I saw—and loved you—I believed
    A certain crisis in my life was passed.
Deceiving you, I was myself deceived,
    Trusting the last misfortune was the last:
    And still I held that fond delusion fast,
And would not think what shadow of strange fate
Lay on my life, until it was too late!

"All unprepared, you justly were offended,
    And filled, I know, with needless pain and dread.
Now once again I think my troubles ended,
    And laid forever with the silent dead.
    Still let me say what then I should have said;
And guard the future, if in spite of all
Precautions, evil should again befall."

His trembling fingers for a moment flitted
    Across his brow; and mind and frame were shaken;
Till, half-forgetting her own wrongs, she pitied
    His greater woe, and felt her love rewaken.
    "O, why was I so cruelly forsaken?
Left, a weak woman, in a land of strangers,
Exposed"—she thought of Robert—"to such dangers!

"But that—all that—is now beyond recall.
    You too have suffered—O for what, from whom?

All is forgiven, if you will tell me all!"
　　He turned away, and rose, and walked the room,
　　Upon his front a thunder-cloud of gloom,
And a portentous trouble in his eye;
Then paused, with downcast looks, and made reply.

"The cause," he faltered, "never can be told;
　　We must not talk of that!" Florinda felt
Her heart grow suddenly all stony-cold,
　　Which love and pity had begun to melt.
　　"It was a dark necessity which dealt
So sternly with us both: should you outlive me,
You may know all,—and then you will forgive me."

He sank upon a chair, and once more covered
　　His changing visage, now convulsed and wan,
Where something of the awful anguish hovered,
　　Which art has fixed immovably upon
　　The deathless marble of Laocoön.
Alarmed she turned, appearing not to heed it;
And, after a brief struggle, he proceeded.

"Ask not the cause; but should there come a time,
　　When I once more may be compelled to leave you,
Account not my necessity a crime;
　　Nor deem that I would willingly deceive you;
　　Nor let my going, nor my silence, grieve you;
But bear my absence—which can never be
So sad to you as terrible to me!

"That such a time may never come again,
　　I do devoutly hope! But it is just
That you should know; then if it comes—O then"—
　　He lifted wide, imploring eyes—"you must—
　　You *will* support me with your love and trust!
Let me, unquestioned, go and come at will:
For only so can we be happy still!"

VII

So earnest was he, and so well she knew
    It would be vain and cruel to prolong
The pain of that unhappy interview,
    That, though her curiosity was strong,
    And deep the old resentful sense of wrong,—
Two things with which the unregenerate heart
Is apt to find it rather hard to part;—

And though not much a heroine, she rose
    Heroically to the situation,
And, prudently forbearing to oppose
    Profitless question or expostulation
    To these hard terms of reconciliation,
Bowed her proud will, as do the wise,—or just
As you and I do, when we find we must.

She yielded, and immediately repented,
    Foreseeing endless mystery, doubt, and slander.
Nor can I say that she was quite contented,
    When Vernon told her, with surprising candor,
    "For your sake, I have banished Alexander;
Though, to relieve my mind of many cares,
I still must let him manage my affairs."

Which somehow did not please her altogether.
    But now the maid approached once more, to say
The coachman at the door demanded whether
    She wished the carriage ordered, still to stay.
    "Why, no!" she answered; "send the man away."
While sundry recollections rushing over her,
With quick, confusing blushes seemed to cover her.

Ah, well her reäwakened soul might shrink
    From the great peril that so late impended!
She shuddered at herself; and feared to think
    How differently the morning might have ended,
    If all had happened as she first intended;

What misery and remorse might now await her,
Had Vernon but arrived a minute later.

So slight a finger-post of circumstance
    May turn one's fate! But to the soul, the savor
Of virtue saved, though saved by seeming chance,
    And though it have a certain homely flavor,
    Is sweet to taste, and sweeter grows forever!
While sin, so pleasant in the hour's swift haste,
Is biting-bitter to the after-taste.

She felt the joy of rescued rectitude;
    And from the rankling cinders of regret
Rose heavenward the pure flame of gratitude
    For her deliverance; making her forget
    What unseen Woe might walk beside her yet:
Her husband she regarded as her savior
From her own wayward heart and weak behavior.

The long-lost bridegroom's cloudy brow soon cleared,
    And even Florinda found new hope and peace
In their reunion. Then the Aunt appeared,
    Flushed from the street, asthmatic and obese,
    And welcomed home the husband of her niece,
With rapture: nothing could exceed the dear Aunt's
Surprise and pleasure at his reappearance.

VIII

Public opinion, having had satiety
    Of adverse gossip, now began to waver.
Vernon had come! and once more Good Society
    Inclined to take Florinda into favor.
    Those who had wronged her graciously forgave her,
And, having spread the scandal, or received it,
Loudly declared that they had not believed it.

Vernon's return had virtually acquitted her
    Of every fault,—those wary ones reflected.

So, having wounded, they came round and pitied her;
    And it was Vernon's turn to be suspected—
    A man who had so shamefully neglected
That sadly injured and long-suffering one,—
As it appeared, for nothing she had done.

But women—and the world—condone in men
    What they condemn in women without charity.
And so when Vernon blossomed out again,
    A fashion-flower of such distinguished rarity,
    After his recent slight irregularity
Of conduct,—he was marvelled at, admired,
Gossiped about, and all the more desired.

If men have manners, never mind their morals!
    And do not make too close investigation
Into the intrigues and domestic quarrels
    Of such as hold high cards of wealth and station:
    Why pass with scorn, or view with indignation,
Or anything so impolite as passion,
A gentleman of fortune, or of fashion?

Society is full of politic,
    Smooth people, courteous, shunning all dissension,
Who, should they find even Judas in their clique,
    Well-dressed, would treat him with polite attention,
    And hardly think it worth the while to mention
That most unfortunate misunderstanding
He is reported to have had a hand in.

Behind this stucco of the world's politeness,
    I find some moral framework not amiss,
To give the social fabric strength and lightness.
    The sculptured forms of strong, fair courtesies
    Uphold while they adorn the edifice;
Like Caryatides, whose true intent
Is strength and grace,—support and ornament.

GEORGE PARSONS LATHROP

Part V

Husband and Lover

I

I do not say that Guy was to be sorted
    With wretches guilty of some heinous treason;
Only that he was quite absurdly courted—
    To his annoyance: partly for which reason
    He hurried to the mountains for a season,
With Mrs. Vernon,—to piece on a truer
And happier ending to their bridal tour.

Happier no doubt it was; and yet not wholly
    Happy for either. Vernon was oppressed
By a persistent, gentle melancholy:
    It seemed as if the world within his breast
    Were, like the peaceful world without, possessed
By the sad spirit of the early Fall,
Which in a pensive haze enveloped all.

Florinda's heart still suffered from the sense
    Of hidden wrong,—a constant, slow corroding;
Seeking for sympathy and confidence,
    She met the shadow of a vague foreboding;
    And felt, beside, the ceaseless, secret goading
Of her own conscience, and the thought of Lorne,—
Deep in her heart an ever-present thorn.

Moreover, she this startling fact discovered,—
    Saturn was never very far away!
Wherever they might be, around them hovered
    The banished Varlet, like a bird of prey.
    He came on business; but he seemed to stay
For pleasure; and she knew that Guy conferred
In secresy with that forbidden bird.

Which state of things she could at last endure
　　No longer. "I entreat you, dear," she cried,
"Take back the man—you need him, I am sure—
　　For my sake! I shall not be satisfied
　　Until you do." But Vernon smiled and sighed.
"I do not need him very much, I find,—
Save now and then. But you are very kind."

Her pent-up passion now began to surge
　　Within her, overleaping all discretion;
And pain and penitence combined to urge
　　Her desperately on to make confession
　　Of her first fault and subsequent transgression,—
In the wild hope that he might make as ample
A revelation, following her example.

II

Beside a torrent, on a great gray boulder,
　　They rested, in a little paradise
Of wood and stream: her hand was on his shoulder;
　　And full on him she turned her troubled eyes,
　　Deep as the pools, reflecting deep blue skies,
That trembled near them, fringed by the long lashes
Of curved birch boughs and overleaning ashes.

"O, will you let me speak? I cannot bear
　　This coldness and reserve!"—A quick flush came
Into his cheek.—"Dear, if we cannot share
　　Each other's sorrows, even each other's shame,
　　I feel that we are married but in name,
And all our hopes of happiness must fail!"
The quick flush vanished, and his cheek grew pale.

Her loosened scarf was trailing in the current,
　　Fallen from her arm unheeded. Wildly blended
With the tumultuous voices of the torrent,
　　Thrillingly eloquent her own ascended
　　The gamut of strong passion, till she ended

With accusation of herself, and spoke
Of Lorne, when sobs convulsed her, and it broke.

III

Thereupon Vernon, who sat strangely pallid,
　　Finding her theme was not just what he feared,
Though leading towards that danger, quickly rallied,
　　And (miracle of married men!) appeared
　　Quite unaccountably relieved and cheered,
As if her fault gave life an added flavor,
And she had really rendered him a favor.

She recommended her story; but before
　　She could make full confession, he broke in:
"You will but give me pain by telling more!
　　Whatever your imprudence may have been,
　　I know you have been guilty of no sin.
You may have erred in wisdom, not in virtue;
That is yourself, and never could desert you."

She tried to speak, but still he would not hear her.
　　"There's no true marriage without trust!" said he.
"My perfect faith in you is as a mirror,
　　In which your white unsullied soul I see.
　　If you but have the same high trust in me,—
Which 'tis my life's endeavor to deserve,—
We shall not feel this coldness and reserve.

"Obedience to this law alone secures
　　True wedded bliss.—This Robert I must know,
And he shall be my friend, as he is yours.
　　And like this mountain stream our life shall flow,
　　As bright and happy"—Here she quite let go
The scarf her hand unconsciously was trailing,
Which off upon the whirling stream went sailing.

Away it floated, light as any feather;
　　And he, before the waves could wholly wet it,

Reckless alike of health and patent leather,
    With a resounding splash, jumped in to get it;
    Less like a husband who might well have let it
Await some prudent action, than a lover,
Who for a glove would have gone in all over.

The conversation, which was interrupted,
    Was not resumed; and Vernon did not learn
How far Florinda's heart had been corrupted;
    Nor did he show thereat the least concern
    Or after-thought; save that, on their return
From travel, he reminded her to send
Some sort of invitation to her friend.

IV

A fine surprise, meanwhile—which we must mention—
    Awaited her; and happily expressed
The tender husband's delicate attention,
    Not only to her worldly interest,
    But to her lightest fancies, known or guessed.
Out driving, they drew up before a brown
Stone front, one day, on their return to town;

And with a princeliness that had no precedence
    Even in his princely conduct, Vernon there
Presented her a charming city residence,
    Finished and furnished with the greatest care,
    And filled with objects elegant and rare;
All in accordance with her utmost wishes,
Even to the monogram upon the dishes.

"All's yours": he put a package in her hand:
    "These are insurance papers and the deed."
"O, now," she said, "I think I understand!"
    Seeing just then, with eyes too dim to read,
    From the back stairs a swarthy face recede,
With points to its mustaches, and a pattern
Of necktie that reminded her of Saturn.

GEORGE PARSONS LATHROP

It was a jewel of a house; in short,
    The very place where one might hope to drown
Memories and cares of an uncanny sort,
    And set one's self serenely to live down
    Evil reports about one in the town,—
An easy matter in a neat, brown-stone,
Luxurious little mansion of one's own.

Fair fortune is a magic cloak, which renders
    Invisible the foibles of the wearer;
And like a lovely setting, outward splendors
    To dazzled eyes make what is fair seem fairer;
    While loads of wealth no more exalt the bearer
Unskilled in its fine uses, than the pack
Of costly goods upon an ass's back.

The Vernons were not of this vulgar class;
    But polished ease and elegance of place
Seemed native to them, as the lakelet's glass
    To the swan's form and duplicated grace.
    To their grand house thronged Flattery and Grimace;
And it became the favorite resort
Of a small circle of the better sort.

V

Of these was Lorne, who nobly had subdued
    His heart meanwhile to sweet self-sacrifice
And aspiration for his lady's good;
    So that he now appeared to casual eyes
    No more Florinda's friend than he was Guy's.
Blessed, if not happy, in a book of songs
He forged his fancies and forgot his wrongs.

He always saw the husband with the wife;
    And him he studied with a most devout
Desire to solve the mystery of his life;
    But found not even a thread to ravel out.
    He went but seldom,—wisely I've no doubt;

Though Vernon always met him with a glow
Of welcome which Florinda did not show.

And was *she* happy? Well, at least she seemed so,
    And that was something: often we care less
For really being so, than being deemed so,
    And better bear the loss of happiness
    Than the world's comment on our ill success:
Rather will Pride relinquish every vestige
Of honest substance, than the phantom, prestige.

Still something of this pride survived in her,
    In spite of suffering and humiliation;
And served to mould and finish, as it were,
    That placid mien and perfect modulation
    Of smile and speech, that so became her station,
And masked in manners exquisitely charming,
None guessed what thoughts distressful or alarming.

Her fame was fair, her beauty shone full-orbed,
    'Mid diamond stars and luminous clouds of shawls
And laces: time and thought seemed all absorbed
    In dressing and undressing, making calls,
    In dinners, drives, receptions, operas, balls;
To cope with which, in all their gay confusion,
Argues, if not great sense, some constitution.

Vernon was ever ready to escort her
    In all these rounds of fashionable folly,—
In nothing would her loving husband thwart her,—
    Although he had not yet recovered wholly
    From his late, strange, autumnal melancholy:
Far from attempting selfishly to stay it, he
Joined with her in the giddy whirl of gayety.

VI

A truer solace in the mind's resources
    Lorne had meanwhile. There is a correlation

Of spiritual as of material forces:
    The passions which we waste in dissipation,
    Swayed by the soul are tides of inspiration;
And the same power that devastates the bosom
With tempests, reappears in bud and blossom.

To reach somehow the good all men aspire;
    But in our ignorance and impatience, we
Encounter countless ills; and find that fire,
    Which comforts, also will consume. Ah me!
    How beautiful some broken lives might be,
Did only mild and sane desires attend us,
And not the overpowering and tremendous!

While love, debased, is like the prophet's rod,
    Which changed into a serpent on the ground,
Exalted, 't is the noblest gift of God,
    By beams of potent influence ring'd around.
    With something of this glory Lorne was crowned,
Which rayed a subtle light into his look,
And played about the pages of his book.

All things he saw as symbols, in a splendor
    Of beauty and bright meanings not their own.
There walked with him a Presence sweet and tender,
    By an unwonted light and joy made known,
    So that when loneliest he was least alone;
Tasting that ecstasy, or something near it,
Which saints have in the presence of the Spirit.

It seemed as if the staid old Universe,
    Moved by a more than Orphean inspiration,
Did reel and dance into his joyous verse;
    And it were all the business of Creation
    To masquerade to his imagination,
In fleeting shapes, through whose thin veils he saw
The gray old verities of Life and Law.

Where is the key to this divine condition?
    What is the flame that, touching brow and lips,
Confers the poet's power of speech and vision?
    Or leaves him in mysterious, dull eclipse,
    When neither toil nor prayer, nor all the whips
And scourges of the conscience and the will,
Can bring again the vision and the thrill!

In solitude, or in the busy street,
    Almost without his choice or his endeavor,
His songs sung to him, and he found them sweet,
    So sweet and varied, that it seemed they never
    Might cease again, but so sing on forever!—
A possibility which looms appalling,
In some who have the choice and not the calling.

Strange seemed sometimes the sound of his own name,
    An echo of some far-off memory!
But from Florinda now a summons came,
    That broke this bubble of bright ecstasy.
    "For my sake, for my husband's, come to me!"
She wrote,—or words of like portentous presage;
And off went Lorne, obedient to the message.

VII

As he was hasting down Broadway, before
    The entrance to a showy lodging-house
He spied a coach, into whose open door
    With most dejected mien and haggard brows
    Stepped Vernon; while with deprecating bows
A gay mulatto gently pressed him through,
Then quickly followed, and the door clapped to.

"Saturn, by Heaven!" thought Rob, as off they sped.
    It happened in a moment; but this chance
To the astonished Lorne interpreted
    Florinda's business with him in advance;
    For it had taken but a passing glance

To see in Vernon's singular appearance
Something that called for friendly interference.

He hurried to the house. He had not seen her
    For many days, and was dismayed to find
How changed she was in feature and demeanor,—
    Frantic in action and half-crazed in mind;
    For, meeting him, she left her mask behind;
And flung herself before him with a cry,
Grief in her speech and frenzy in her eye.

VIII

"O Rob!" she cried, "I have no friend but you!
    And you must help me—for no other can!"
"I know," he said: "he's gone! What can I do?"
    "Oh! if you could have seen him when he ran
    Shrieking away—'O save me from that man!'
But it was sadder still to see him cower
And yield,—when Saturn had him in his power,—

"And coldly thrust me off, and hear him say
    He went of his own will! It is not so!
That dreadful man has taken him away
    For his own selfish ends—which I will know!
    If ever you would serve me, Robert, go!
Follow that fiend, before it is too late,
And save my husband from some horrid fate!"

Lorne tells what he has seen: yet small the hope
    That ever he can get on Saturn's trace:
And how can one like him expect to cope
    With a great villain of such crafty ways?
    Still, eager to assist her, he obeys;
Receives her blessing in their brief adieux,—
And money, which he cannot well refuse.

No sooner left alone than, recollecting
    What Guy before had told her of his going,

Which was not to be questioned; and reflecting
    How much more fatal sometimes is the knowing
    Of hidden things than all the evil growing
Out of the things themselves while they are hidden;
And what a thankless errand she had bidden

Her friend perform,—she wished to call him back;
    But quieted her conscience with the thought
That he could hardly get upon their track,—
    That they who had so many times been sought
    Vainly by others, were not to be caught.
Then in a strong revulsion of distress,
Clasping wild hands, she prayed for his success.

Part VI

SATURN

I

Lorne undertook the business with a zeal
    And promptness hardly to have been expected.
The lodging-house had little to reveal,
    And yet one clew that Saturn had neglected
    Showed where his baggage went, and where he checked it
For a swift western train that afternoon,—
Which Lorne, this point decided, followed soon.

And now commenced the rather curious chase
    Of the escaping husband by the lover.
'Mid crossing trains Lorne often lost the trace
    Whereby he hoped to hunt the pair to cover,
    Which happy chances helped him to recover,—
A friendly clerk or baggageman, somewhere,
Remembering Saturn's face and foppish air.

At last he seemed to lose it altogether
    Upon the Mississippi; where he stayed
His course at Memphis, undecided whether
    He should go back or forward. Here he strayed
    One afternoon along the esplanade
And high bluff of the river-fronting town,
To watch the boats and see the sun go down.

The lyric fit had left him; but the sight
    Of the strong river sweeping vast and slow,
Gleaming far off, a flood of crimson light;
    And, darkly hung between it and the glow
    Of a most lovely sunset sky, the low,
Interminable forests of Arkansas,
Might have inspired some very pretty stanzas.

The esplanade looks down upon the landing,
    A broadly shelving bank, well-trodden and bare,
Called by a singular misunderstanding
    The *levee*,—while there is no levee there;
    The famous landing at New Orleans, where
There *is* one, having fixed the name forever
For that and other landings on the river.

Acres of merchandise, of cotton-bales,
    And bales of hay, awaiting transportation;
Ploughs, household goods, and kegs of rum or nails,
    Endless supplies for village and plantation,
    Enclosed a scene of wondrous animation,
Of outcry and apparent wild confusion
Contrasting with the sunset's soft illusion;—

The steamers lying broadside to the stream,
    With delicately pillared decks, the clang
Of bells, the uproar of escaping steam;
    There, tugging at some heavy rope, the gang
    Of slaves that all together swayed and sang,
Their voices rising in a wild, rich chime,
To which lithe forms and lithe black arms kept time;

The shouts of negro-drivers, droves of mules,
    Driven in their turn by madly yelling blacks;
Chairs, tables, kitchen-ware and farming-tools,
    Carts, wagons, barrels, boxes, bales, and sacks,
    Pushed, hauled, rolled, tumbled, tossed, or borne on backs
Of files of men, across the ways of plank
Between the loading steamers and the bank!

Then as the sunlight faded from the stream,
    And deepening shadows cooled the upper air,
The waves were lighted by the lurid gleam
    Of flambeaux that began to smoke and flare,
    And cast a picturesque and ruddy glare
On shore and boats and men of every hue—
Among the rest, a face that Robert knew.

He had strolled down upon the bank to note
    The arrival of a steamer and await
The travellers disembarking from the boat;
    When from the gangway, on through rows of freight,
    In the red glare advanced that face of fate,—
Swart features of the alert and powerful sort,
Although a dandy's: Saturn's face, in short.

Lorne's heart leaped to his lips, and he was tempted
    To clutch the rascal without more ado,—
A rather risky feat to have attempted,
    For Saturn was the stouter of the two;
    And always 'tis a thing that you will rue,
So to unmask your purpose, unprepared
To close and finish with the game you've scared.

He looked for Vernon: Saturn came alone,
    Bearing a light portmanteau, which he flung
At a black coachman; whose white eyeballs shone
    And ivories grinned, as off he marched among
    The less distinguished drivers, open swung
His carriage door, and dashed it to again,
Then perched upon his box with whip and rein:

Saturn inside and Lorne on foot without!
    Here was a crisis: what was to be done?
No moment to be wasted in weak doubt:
    Follow he must,—but should he ride or run?
    There were the drivers: he selected one,
And straightway mounted with him to his seat:
Money makes coachmen kind and horses fleet.

'Mid drays and piles of freight their way they find.
    "What street, my friend?"—"Follow that coach!"—"All right!"
The glare of flambeaux quickly fades behind,
    And through the suburbs, on into the night
    (Keeping the coach they followed well in sight),

With rattling speed (the ways were dim and rough),
They bowled along the summit of the bluff.

The mighty river glimmered far below,
    Soon lost to view; while on the other hand,
Just breaking from the horizon, looming slow,
    The red moon, burning like a red bright brand,
    Far over misty levels of dim land
And scattered roofs and gardens shone, and showed
The forward coach drawn up beside the road.

III

With columned front and roof of gleaming slate,
    A dim house stood half hid in trees, surrounded
By a high wall. Before a high close gate,
    Down from his box the dandy's coachman bounded,
    And pulled a bell, whose iron clangor sounded
Hollow within: then straightway open flew
The double panels, while the coach drove through;

And closed again behind with sullen clank,
    Just as the second coach drove slowly by,—
Shutting their ponderous jaws of bolted plank
    Forbiddingly; appearing to defy
    Alike marauding force and prying eye.
Then with the brightening moonlight seemed to fall
A deep mysterious silence over all.

Thought Lorne, "I've tracked the devil to his den!—
    What house is that?"—The driver turned to stare,
(One of your dry, deliberative men,
    With a wise drawl), and answered with an air
    Of cautious candor: "Friend, you have me there!
That house has got a sort of secret history,—
Leastwise a curious nickname—'Castle Mystery.'"

                                                GEORGE PARSONS LATHROP

IV

"Who owns the place?"—"That's more than I can tell.
    Most of the time nobody but an old,
Queer cove ties up here; while the master—well,
    Just there comes in the mystery; I've been told
    He practises the art of making gold.
He spends a powerful heap when he's away;
That gone, he comes and makes some more, they say."

"But that's a foolish fable!"—"Yes, of course;
    Some sort of counterfeiting game, perhaps;
Unnatural stories have some natural source.
    The old man helps; he keeps the tools and traps;—
    Beats all your deep philosophizing chaps!
Doctor, he's called: he may be: but the fact is,
He's all gone up and run to seed in practice.

"He has a room and shop plumb full of books,
    Vials and things; and studies day and night,
And tries experiments, until he looks
    Dazed, like an owl that's brought too near the light:
    Keeps that black coachman, and one servant,—white;
And now and then there comes a strutting fellow
That's neither black nor white, but mongrel yellow.

"He's in the coach there now—or was. Some say
    He owns the place. That's their imagination;
And all because he has a pompous way,
    As if he had a mortgage on Creation
    In his breast-pocket. That's my observation.
I've seen him come and go, and then—it's queer!
Sometimes he won't be round here for a year.

"Well, no; I never had the luck to see
    The master,—he keeps mighty close, somehow.
He's the last person you would take to be
    A rogue, by what they tell me. I allow,
    He's at his business in the house there now;—

He hates it bad enough, but has to do it,
As if some fate or devil drove him to it."

Lorne sought in vain the root of this uncouth,
    Fabulous story. Error is a vine,
A parasite upon the tree of Truth,
    About whose modest stem its own malign,
    Luxurious branches sometimes twist and twine,
Until it seems a hopeless task to single
The true from false, their boughs so mix and mingle.

V

Back by the house they drove. An open field
    Adjoined the "Castle" grounds, and bounded all.
Eager to see what its gray stones concealed,
    Lorne rode into the shadow of the wall,
    Rose to his feet, and—being somewhat tall—
Looked over, while his heart beat high and fast,
Into Guy Vernon's strange retreat at last;

Nearing the scene of mystery with a thrill.
    There lay the garden, half in shadow bound,
Half-silvered by the moonlight soft and still,
    Slanting on tree and shrub and cultured ground,
    Where many a path and peaceful alley wound;
All perfumed by the breath of early spring.
The tender bud and first sweet blossoming.

Before the quiet garden stood the solemn,
    Pale-fronted mansion; its broad, silent mass
Projecting from quaint gable and pale column
    A vast and shapeless shadow on the grass:
    One warm, bright light behind tall doors of glass,
Which opened from a cheerful banquet-room
On the dark lawn and ray-besprinkled gloom.

VI

There, like the lord and master of the Castle,
 A petty despot, at his meat and wine,
Alone, sat Saturn; while an abject vassal
 Stood by to serve his dish and see him dine.
 Lorne could even see the rings and trinkets shine,
As, blazing there in his own solitary
Magnificence, he ate, and sipped his sherry.

Soon, having finished his repast, the Varlet
 Wiped his mustache and gave the ends a pull;
Then set a smoking-cap of flaming scarlet,
 With gorgeous tassels, on his carded wool;
 Lit a cigar, and out upon the cool
Veranda stepped, while from the open door
His own burlesquing shadow stretched before.

A base act Robert scorned; and when he saw
 Saturn face towards him, all at once he thought
It would be highly proper to withdraw,—
 Not just because he dreaded to be caught
 Playing the spy; but to the ill-doer naught
Conduces more to virtuous reflection,
Than a good, startling prospect of detection.

And yet there was a fearful fascination
 In spying out the stronghold of the foe.
Had he not come with stern determination
 To track, to watch, to circumvent, to know
 The villain's plots, then strike some sudden blow
To rescue Vernon, or at least determine
The cause of his subjection to such vermin?

He would have willingly become a pupil
 Of Machiavel himself, but to enhance
Florinda's happiness; and should he scruple
 To take advantage now of any chance
 Which served his righteous purpose to advance?

It seemed as if the hand of mighty Nemesis
Had led him thus to the mysterious premises.

He stooped in shadow, but did not retire:
    Hand grasping wall, and trembling knee the coach,
He crouched; when from the Castle rose a dire,
    Deep outcry of entreaty and reproach;
    And, springing to his feet, he saw approach—
While Saturn turned with cool, sarcastic grin—
Florinda's husband, rushing from within!

VII

Guy Vernon, most astonishingly clad:
    In leather apron, bare arms; on his head
A paper cap; in his right hand he had
    A sort of ladle; features flushed and red,
    As from a furnace whence he just had fled.
A lean, slight figure followed, with lank face,—
The little owl-eyed Doctor of the place.

In tones of strong remonstrance and entreaty
    Vernon addressed the Varlet; who stood by
Without a flicker of remorse or pity
    In the cold, settled purpose of his eye,
    And waved him back: then with a plaintive cry
To the freed slave knelt the subjected freeman,
The sad, fallen man to the exalted demon!

For so it seemed to Lorne: which when he saw,
    His fury he no longer could restrain.
Reckless of danger, dignity, or law,
    Or how the outer world he should regain,
    From coach to high wall-top he leaped amain,
Dropped down within,—a sheer ten-foot descent,—
And through the shaded shrubbery crashing went

To lawn, veranda, and wide-open casement;
    And stood, one fiery pulse from head to foot,

Before the Varlet turning with amazement,
    Guy Vernon staggering back irresolute,
    And the lean Doctor blinking pale and mute;
While his astonished coachman, at the wall,
Peered over in blank wonder at it all.

Lorne eagerly reached forth his hand for Guy's:
    "Vernon! my friend!"—But Saturn, all serene,
Having recovered from his first surprise,
    With a polite "Excuse me!" stepped between:
    "I do not know you, sir!" with courteous mien
Barring the way. "My Master is engaged."
Whereat Lorne opened on him, all enraged.

"I know *you*, Alexander,—Dandy Sam—
    Saturn or Satan,—what's your name? no matter!"
The Varlet made his wonderful salaam,
    And quirked his eyebrows with a leer: "You flatter!"
    Preventing still Lorne's progress; while the latter
Called vainly after Guy,—who shrank away
In sad confusion,—charging him to stay.

"I've come for you—I will not go without you!
    Think of Florinda!—all shall yet be well!
What is this net which they have woven about you?
    Where is your manhood? Break this hideous spell!"
    And Lorne, regardless of a spring and yell
From Saturn, made a dash, the table cleared—
Too late! already Guy had disappeared.

With him, the Doctor; and behind them both
    The obsequious servant had secured the door.
Lorne turned on Saturn; with a thrilling oath,
    And look more threatening than his speech, he swore
    Not to depart from out that house before
He had conferred with Vernon. "Then I fear
You will stay late!" said Saturn with a leer.

"You cannot turn me out—I will not stir!
    I am commissioned by his injured wife;
And I will take her husband back to her,
    Or make you a frank present of my life!"
    And, all unarmed, Lorne looked full-armed for strife.
There was a moment's awkward silence; then
The lordly Saturn was himself again.

VIII

He turned magnificently to his henchman,—
    Who seemed, in vulgar terms, a sort of cook
And general waiting-man; a stocky Frenchman,
    Servile, alert, intelligent; who took
    His orders from a signal or a look,
And vanished. Saturn blandly smiled. "You're right!
You shall be satisfied this very night!

"Be seated!"—with elaborate politeness.
    "You shall be welcome as the lady's friend.
I'm sorry that she questions my uprightness:
    You share her prejudice, I apprehend!—
    Here's some refreshment I can recommend."
The nimble Frenchman placed upon the table
A bottle with an interesting label;

And poured a glass, which Lorne declined. "No harm, sir!"
    Said Saturn with a smile. "I know my place;
So there is no occasion for alarm, sir;
    I am too well aware of the disgrace
    For gentlemen of your superior race
To drink and fellowship with one of mine.
But there's no taint of color in the wine!"

IX

Which sarcasm made Lorne wince. He was a man
    Who hated from his heart all tyranny
Of artificial caste and social ban;

In broad, imaginative sympathy
A poet; for, however they may be
Wanting in social manners and urbanity,
Poets are all for freedom and humanity.

"That you have been a servant, or in slavery,
Or have a colored skin," he cried, "who cares?
Not I! But I have small respect for knavery,
Foppish magnificence and insolent airs!"
At which plain English Saturn grins and glares.
"You're frank! But 'tis just possible that you
May not see all things, from your point of view.

"What you have called my knavery, in your haste—
Of that there's something more for you to know.
Then please set down to differences of taste,
And my unhappy race's love of show,
Much of the foppery that disgusts you so;
And it may be the insolence you've noticed
Is just a proud but ignorant person's protest

"Against injustice which would keep him under,—
Too violent a rebound of self-respect.
That I am what I am, is no great wonder:
No fine advantages, please recollect,
Of birth and education." Which direct
And simple speech took Robert by surprise,
And brought a curious twinkle to his eyes.

"That Mr. Vernon's lady deemed that I
Was his bad genius, I was well aware.
But it was not convenient to deny
What none the less was somewhat hard to bear.
No doubt I've acted strangely in the affair;
But I have been no more the evil cause,
Than whirlwinds are produced by whirling straws.

"And neither is my master a great villain:
Our weak point lies in his too strict veracity.

With something to conceal, he was not willing
    To use a little innocent mendacity,—
    Of which I have perhaps a small capacity;
Enough to have invented some slight fiction,
Which would have saved his lady much affliction.

"Don't think my influence over him lies solely
    In his great fear to have his trouble known.
For thirty years, sir, he has trusted wholly
    To my fidelity: I am proud to own,
    That in our boyhood, before he had grown
Familiar with misfortune and disaster,
I was his servant, he my little master.

"Then when affliction came, our ties were closer.
    I shared his fortunes; sleeping or awake,
I was his chosen attendant. You must know, sir,
    The ancient family honor was at stake.
    There was no sacrifice they would not make—
Honest device they would not try—to hide
The stain upon the old Virginia pride.

"With Master Guy himself the constant dread
    Of an exposure had become a steady
Motive and habit, when at last it led
    To the deception practised on his lady.
    We hoped,—and he believed—that he already
Had passed the crisis,—that his chains were broken."
Lorne started wonderingly, and would have spoken.

Saturn proceeded: "Since you've found us here,
    And got some partial facts in your possession,
And are the lady's agent, and appear
    A gentleman of sense and good discretion,
    I shall go on and make a frank confession
Of the main circumstance—which you have guessed?—
Then we shall make short business with the rest.

"This place was fitted for his occupation,
    At my suggestion, and with his consent.
Then, when he felt the first faint intimation,—
    The coming of the terrible event,—
    To keep his secret he was well content
To fly with me, and in this shelter wait
Until the storm was over. But of late,

"Love for his lady, fear to do her wrong,
    And hope that still the shadow might pass by,
Has caused my master to delay too long.
    But, though I was not pleasing to her eye,
    Which had to be avoided, I was nigh,
And watched him close, and when all hope was past,
Of his improvement, brought him off at last.

"Our Doctor was the family physician;
    Under his charge my master first was placed.
Then he was offered here, in this position,
    Advantages he readily embraced;
    Where undisturbed he can indulge his taste
For chemistry, until some fresh attack
Of the disorder brings his patient back.

"'Tis now twelve years since my old master died,
    And left him and his fortune to my care.
The mother went before. We have three tried
    And faithful servants, who would neither dare
    To tell his secret, nor to hurt a hair
Of that dear head!" Here, winking hard, the dandy,
With a fierce gulp, tossed off a glass of brandy.

"I showed some rudeness, which you'll please excuse.
    An ignorant man is liable to err.
Now shall you care to see him? As you choose.
    In any case, I do not fancy, sir,
    That you will wish to take him back to her!
The thing has gone so far, though, I suppose
It will perhaps be better if she knows.

"Sometimes for several years he is exempt;
　　Then the old indications: first, a strange
Irritability; then perhaps the attempt
　　To hide even from himself the coming change
　　In a forced gayety; then the symptoms range
From moody melancholy and fitful sadness
To deep despondency and downright madness!

"Quite harmless; often fancies he is poor,
　　But that he has the art of making gold.
Indulgence is the surest way to cure
　　His whims; and 'tis a comfort to behold
　　Even a poor madman flattered and consoled.
But when he knelt tonight and begged for snow
To make some silver, I had none to show."

X

So Saturn told his story; and 'tis time
　　Mine, too, were ended,—which so far has strayed,
Winding along the indented shores of rhyme,
　　In many an idle pool and eddy played.—
　　Lorne did not keep the promise he had made,
But all alone, and sorrowful, and late,
That night, took his departure by the gate.

To know the worst is better than long doubt,
　　The slow, consuming fever of suspense.
Therefore, when Lorne had traced the mystery out,
　　And to Florinda bore the news, a sense
　　Of soothing respite followed long, intense
Horror and dread, and speedily allayed
The anguish of the wound the sharp truth made.

That some remorse for her unjust suspicion
　　Of Saturn stung her, cannot be denied.
Then came a message sent by Guy's physician;
　　And questions rose of duty, love, and pride,
　　Which Robert nobly helped her to decide;

And soon she made a journey,—by her presence
To cheer Guy Vernon in his convalescence.

The wise, who would expel a spectral thing
　　That haunts the chambers of the lonely mind,
Invite sweet sound and sight of birds that sing,
　　And flowers and winds and heavenly beams, to find
　　Freely their way through wide-flung door and blind,
And pure affections, an angelic host,
To fill the rooms and drive away the ghost.

The truth was known; and terror of discovery
　　Swayed Vernon's soul no more as in the past;
And for his mind a more complete recovery
　　And perfect cure seemed possible at last.
　　The cloudy future now was clearing fast,
And would have brought in brighter days, no doubt,
When our unlucky civil war broke out.

There, where the treasure is, the heart will be:
　　Guy Vernon's bride was northern; his estates
And many slaves were in the South; and he,
　　Having in vain withstood the fiery fates
　　That strove to rend the covenant of States,
Went with his own, and helped to fight their battles,
To save his cotton, cane, and human chattels.

His lands were overrun, his slaves were freed,
　　The cause was lost he struggled to defend,
And poor Florinda wore a widow's weed!
　　And now no doubt you think the lover friend
　　Steps in to give our tale a happy end.
But truth is truth; and when the news was carried
To Lorne at last, he had been three years married.

XI

Not his the queen of wit, or star of beauty,
　　Dazzling beholders, but a pearl more precious,

Set in the sacred ring of daily duty;
    Not vast domain, but something far more spacious;
    Nor great renown; yet Fortune has been gracious,
And to requite his simple faith has sent
The all-enclosing freehold of Content.

Smiles of affection keep his fireside bright,
    Around his heart light-footed cherubs dance:
Love and the Muse make labor a delight,
    The spirit blithe, and sweet the countenance.
    Books he has printed, essay, song, romance;
And now—the latest venture of them all—
He publishes a novel in the fall.

O critic of his little book! I hope
    You will not prove of that pedantic class
Who view defects as through a telescope;
    But when they see a modest merit pass,
    Smile, shrug, look doubtful, and reverse the glass,
Then swear the object is so very small
As scarcely to be visible at all.

And take this counsel kindly as I mean it:
    In your reviews, don't hasten to disclose
The story's plot,—before the world has seen it,
    Pulling to pieces one's poor little rose!
    But let its readers—ere the volume goes
To the oblivion of their upper shelves—
Pluck out its little mystery for themselves.

Vain is the mask! Who cannot, at desire,
Name every singer in the hidden choir?
A thin disguise is that which veils with care
The face, but lets the changeless heart lie bare!

A Note About the Author

George Parsons Lathrop (1851–1898) was an American editor, poet, and novelist. Born in Honolulu, he was educated in New York City and Dresden, Germany. After a brief time abroad, he returned to New York to pursue his literary interests. After marrying Rose Hawthorne, the daughter of American novelist Nathaniel Hawthorne, in 1871, Lathrop became the associate editor for the *Atlantic Monthly* and later the *Boston Courier*. In the late 1870s, he worked as an editor for Roberts Brothers, overseeing the publication of such works as *A Masque of Poets* (1878), which compiled the works of several dozen English and American writers. Part of the Boston-based publisher's "No Name" series, *A Masque of Poets* presented the works of little-known writers—including Emily Dickinson—alongside such recognized masters as Christina Rossetti and James Russell Lowell, leaving each poem anonymous to allow the reader to experience the work without thought of reputation. A relatively minor figure in nineteenth century American literature, Lathrop was nevertheless an interesting and industrious man whose personal and professional life brought him in contact with some of the leading artists of the era.

A Note from the Publisher

Spanning many genres, from non-fiction essays to literature classics to children's books and lyric poetry, Mint Edition books showcase the master works of our time in a modern new package. The text is freshly typeset, is clean and easy to read, and features a new note about the author in each volume. Many books also include exclusive new introductory material. Every book boasts a striking new cover, which makes it as appropriate for collecting as it is for gift giving. Mint Edition books are only printed when a reader orders them, so natural resources are not wasted. We're proud that our books are never manufactured in excess and exist only in the exact quantity they need to be read and enjoyed.

bookfinity™

Discover more of your favorite classics with Bookfinity™.

- Track your reading with custom book lists.
- Get great book recommendations for your personalized Reader Type.
- Add reviews for your favorite books.
- AND MUCH MORE!

Visit **bookfinity.com** and take the fun Reader Type quiz to get started.

Enjoy our classic and modern companion pairings!

Classic & Modern

Printed in the USA
CPSIA information can be obtained
at www.ICGtesting.com
JSHW022332140824
68134JS00019B/1435

9 781513 212135